Practise
Advanced Writing

Mary Stephens

Addison Wesley Longman Limited
Edinburgh Gate, Harlow,
Essex CM20 2JE, England
and Associated Companies throughout the world.

© Longman Group UK Limited 1992

First published 1992
Tenth impression 1997

Set in 9/10 Versailles Roman

Produced through Longman Malaysia, ACM

ISBN 0 582 06437 6

421STE
326065

ACKNOWLEDGEMENTS

We are grateful to the following for permission to reproduce copyright material:

Bantam Books a division of Bantam, Doubleday, Dell Publishing Group, Inc for an adapted extract from a review of 'The Exorcist' in *Movies on TV* by Steven H Scheuer; BBC Enterprises Limited for an adapted article 'A Students' Guide to Exam Stress' in *The Radio Times* 3–9.6.89; the author's agent for extracts from 'The Landlady', 'Parson's Pleasure' and 'The Way Up to Heaven' by Roald Dahl from *Kiss Kiss* (Michael Joseph Ltd & Penguin Books Ltd) (c) 1953, 1954, 1958, 1959 Roald Dahl and 'Nunc Dimittis' by Roald Dahl from *Someone Like You* (Penguin Books Ltd); André Deutsch Ltd/Penguin Books Ltd for recipe based on 'Roast leg of lamb' from *British Cooking* by Caroline Conran; Faber & Faber Ltd for adapted extract from 'The Rain Horse' from *Wodwo* by Ted Hughes; Gruner & Jahr (UK) for adapted extracts from articles 'Phil Collins – at face value' by William Hall, on Meryl Streep, 'TV: could you be without it?' by Jill Eckersley and 'Talking Point on Nuclear Power' in *Best* magazine, 28.10.88, 28.4.89, 31.3.89 and 9.6.89; Guardian News Service Ltd for adapted extract from article 'Ambulance Shambles' by Simon Beavis, Patrick Wintour and Gareth Parry in *The Guardian* 24.10.89; IPC Magazines Ltd for adapted extract from article 'Why the Future Must be Green' by David Allsop in *Options* magazine February 1989; IPC Magazines Ltd/ Solo Syndication & Literary Agency Ltd for adapted extract from article 'Go Green!' in *Woman's Own* 24.7.89; News (UK) Ltd for adapted extract from article 'Fairy tale story of whale that thinks a ship is his mother' in *Today* 24.10.89; Southern Newspapers plc for adapted extract from article 'Terror of dog attack' by Andy Martin in *Evening Echo, Bournemouth* June 1989; Syndication International (1986) Ltd for adapted extracts from articles '999 Shambles as Police move in' & 'Bergerac TV Horror Photos Shock Family' in *Daily Mirror* 24.10.89. and 30.10.89; the author, Jo Weedon, for adapted extract from her article 'Are our Zoos cruel?' in *Woman's Own* 14.8.89; World Press Network Ltd for adapted extract from *Mississippi*

Burning Review by Sean French in *Marie Claire* magazine, May 1989.

The idea for the 'news' activity on page 89 came from 'Activity Pack Elementary' by Birt and Fletcher, pub. Edward Arnold.

We are grateful to the following for permission to reproduce copyright material:

Barnaby's Picture Library/H. Kanus for page 52; *Best* magazine/Gruner & Jahr (UK) for page 109 (bottom); Camera Press Ltd for pages 9, 75, 103 (left) and 104 (left); The J Allan Cash Photolibrary for pages 103 (right) and 108; John Birdsall Photography for pages 47 (bottom) and 88; Supplied for artist's reference by Bournemouth Dept. of Tourism & Publicity for page 35 (top); Eurocamp Travel Ltd for page 23 (top); S & R Greenhill for pages 19 (bottom) and 105; Greenpeace/Gleizes for page 95; Kobal Collection for page 61; Peter Lake for page 104 (right); Mail Newspapers PLC/Photo supplied by Solo Syndication for page 45; With permission of Metropolitan Police for page 67 (bottom); Network for pages 19 (top), 47 (top left), 47 (top right), 84 and 109 (top); Reproduced with permission from R.D. Press a registered business name of Reader's Digest (Aust) Pty. Ltd from the book entitled *The Way Things Work* by David Macaulay © Dorling Kindersley Ltd London for page 63 (top); Rex Features for page 6; Copyright RSPB, taken from an information leaflet produced by The Royal Society for the Protection of Birds for page 81; Tim Sebastian/Simon & Schuster/Illustrator George Smith for page 62; *The Spectator* for pages 63 (bottom) and 102; Syndication International for page 87 (right).

We have been unable to trace the copyright holders of the photograph on page 87 (left) and would be grateful for any information to enable us to do so.

Picture Research by Sandie Huskinson-Rolfe (PHOTOSEEKERS)

Illustrations by Shaun Williams

CONTENTS

INTRODUCTION

Practise Advanced Writing is a writing skills book designed for students at post FCE level. It follows on from *Practise Writing*, providing the student with practice in a wide variety of written English, including reports, letters, narratives, descriptions and opinions.

The book is divided into four and six page units, providing double page spreads for ease of use. Each unit has a written model, usually in the form of an authentic text, which is followed by a variety of exercises moving from a general analysis of the text to more specialised language exercises. Although this is a writing skills book, there is plenty of opportunity for oral work, as students are required to engage in a good deal of discussion/role play before they are ready to produce a written text of their own. Emphasis is placed on learner independence and students are encouraged to work out rules for themselves. Each unit ends with a summary box which provides a check for students where necessary and a reminder of the basic types of language/format needed for their written tasks.

Writing a Personal Profile

To start you thinking

Get into groups to discuss these questions.

1 What do you think of current trends in pop/rock music? What sort of music do you like best? Have you got a favourite singer/band?

2 What do you think might be the advantages and disadvantages of life as a rock star? Make your own list and then compare with your group.

A personal profile

Now read the magazine article below, which is a profile of rock star Phil Collins.

When five-year-old Phil Collins was given a little tin drum for Christmas it fired a musical spark which would one day make him one 5 of the wealthiest rock stars in Britain. As a solo artist, he made £22 million in 1985 alone, while a world tour with the group Genesis last year earned him and the other members 10 of the band £10 million each. His army of fans include such figures as Princess Diana and Madonna. Yet despite all this wealth and success, Phil Collins remains quiet-spoken 15 and refreshingly down-to-earth about his music, fame, fans and, of course, his money.

Born on January 30th 1951, Phil seemed destined for a life on the 20 stage. While his father was in charge of an insurance office, his mother managed a theatre school in London. All three of her children had parts in films. When Phil got a part in the 25 London production of 'Oliver', he left school for a career in acting. He was now playing drums at parties and clubs and had begun to write his own songs, secretly hoping that one 30 day this would be his full-time job. Then, in 1975, something happened that changed his life.

It all began when he saw an advertisement for a drummer to join 35 a rock band and found himself taken on by a fledgling[1] group called Genesis. Five years on, when singer Peter Gabriel left to go solo, Phil took over on vocals. Now, with sixteen 40 albums to their credit, Genesis are one of the biggest money-spinning rock bands, appealing to all age groups with their music.

Phil's first marriage ended in divorce, 45 but he and his ex-wife have remained good friends and his children, Joely (16) and Simon (12), spend their summer holidays at his £1.5 million farmhouse in Surrey. He is now 50 married to Jill, a former teacher from California, whom he met in a Los Angeles bar. The problems with his first marriage taught him valuable lessons and he no longer lets the 55 strains of showbusiness affect his personal life.

Nowadays, as well as his family, Phil has a number of commitments outside Genesis. These include his 60 solo career, recording with other artists like Eric Clapton, and working to help underprivileged young people with Prince Charles's Trust Committee. In 1988 he launched his 65 acting career, starring in the film 'Buster' to critical acclaim.

Despite all this success, Phil has not changed. He remains as insecure as most of us, and takes care not to 70 squander[2] his money, fearing that hard times may be just down the road. Yet it is hard to imagine what could ever touch the Collins magic carpet of success.

[1]*fledgling*: young, inexperienced
[2]*squander*: waste

Format

With your partner, decide what you think is the topic of each of the paragraphs in the model text. Complete the plan below.

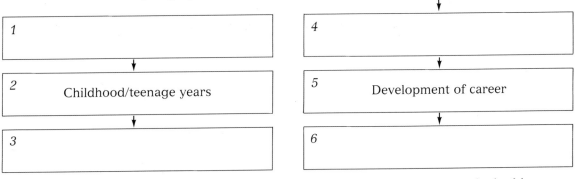

1	4
2 Childhood/teenage years	5 Development of career
3	6

Why do you think the writer has arranged the paragraphs in this particular order?

Linking ideas

A paragraph often has a key idea/sentence which is developed in the rest of the paragraph. The writer may want to give more details, supply quotations, etc. The final sentence often serves as a 'lead in' to the next paragraph.

1 Can you pick out the key sentence in paragraph 2 of the model text?
2 How does the final sentence of paragraph 2 lead in to the following paragraph?
3 Underline any words/phrases in the model text which help to link the paragraphs together.
4 Do you think that the final paragraph 'rounds off' the whole text? Give reasons for your answer.

Using a variety of structures

One of the difficulties of this type of biography writing is lack of variety in sentence structure, for example:

He was born in 1951.
He went to school.
He joined a rock band, etc.

Working in groups, discuss how you would change the following sentences by starting each with one of the words/phrases provided in the box below, for example:

He remains down-to-earth in spite of the fact that he is successful.
a) *Despite* his success, he remains down-to-earth.
b) *Although* he is successful, he remains down-to-earth.

As a result of...	It was through...	After...	Not only...
As well as...	Having...	By...	

1 He left school when he got a part in 'Oliver'.

   a) Having _____
   b) After _____

2 He got his chance with Genesis because he answered an advertisement.

   a) _____
   b) _____

3 He took over vocals when singer Peter Gabriel left to go solo.
   a) _____
   b) _____

4 He now has a variety of projects, including playing with Genesis.
   a) _____
   b) _____

Vocabulary

> **He is quiet and refreshingly down-to-earth.**

Writing a personal profile usually involves describing personal qualities.

1 Can you match the opposites in the following list of adjectives. Use your dictionary to check any words you are unfamiliar with before you begin.

a) outspoken	i) excitable
b) shy/unsure	ii) serious/dour
c) calm	iii) vulnerable
d) impulsive	iv) reticent
e) fun-loving	v) self-conscious
f) guarded	vi) thick-skinned
g) sensitive	vii) out-going
h) tough	viii) forbidding
i) approachable	ix) controlled
j) poised/self-confident	x) open

2 Tick the adjectives above which can be transformed into nouns. Give the noun form for these adjectives, for example:

   calm – calmness

3 Which of the above qualities do you think apply to you? Which qualities do you personally find most attractive in other people? Which do you dislike? Can you add more words to your list?

Tenses

Present perfect or simple past?

These two tenses are usually needed when writing about someone's life.

1 Study the sentences below and, with your partner, work out the rule for when to use each tense.

a) His first marriage *ended* in divorce.
b) Genesis *was formed* in the 1960s.
c) He *has helped* raise millions for charity.
d) He and his ex-wife *have remained* good friends since their divorce.

2 Fill in the blanks in the following sentences using the simple past or present perfect tense of the verbs in the box.

to learn	to take part	to have	to become
to be formed	to be	to work	to go

a) The young Phil Collins _____ a small part in the old Beatles film 'A Hard Day's Night'.
b) Genesis _____ one of the richest rock bands in Britain today.
c) Phil's chauffeur says, 'Out of all the stars I _____ with, he's top of the list!'
d) The rock group _____ at Charterhouse public school in the mid '60s.
e) He _____ remarkable success as a singer/songwriter and now as an actor.

f) Princess Diana _____ a fan some years ago and _____ to see him 'live' several times.

g) He _____ in the 'Live Aid' concert which raised money for famine victims in Africa.

h) Phil _____ in show business almost from the time he could walk, so he _____ to handle the pressure with ease.

Discussion

Discuss the following questions in groups.

1 If you could have dinner tonight with a world-famous person, who would you choose, and why?

2 What would you say are the outstanding personal qualities of the person you have chosen?

3 What do you know about the following areas of their life:

a) childhood?   b) career?   c) family life?

4 What questions would you like to ask them?

5 Which person in your life do you think has influenced you most up to now? Why? Talk to your partner about them.

Writing

Sentence jumble

1 a) The sentences below form the first two paragraphs of a profile of actress Meryl Streep. Work with your partner to put them into the correct order and then write the text out again in two paragraphs. (You may like to copy and cut the text into strips to do this reordering exercise.)

i)	With them she can chuckle at appearing in some of the 'worst-dressed' lists that designers put out when they're looking for cheap publicity.
ii)	Yet, she says: 'I don't believe any of the stuff that people write and say about me, not any of it.'
iii)	'Well', she laughs, 'I can look dreadful! I don't normally wear make-up, anyway.'
iv)	On film, her eyes change colour from blue to green depending on her mood and she can convey a wealth of meaning with just a sideways glance.
v)	However she shuns the spotlight, preferring a quiet evening at home with her family to the Hollywood hype.
vi)	She has, too, a radiant smile that lights up the screen.
vii)	Celebrating her 40th birthday this week, Meryl Streep is one of the screen's most enigmatic and least-known properties.
viii)	This whole look, and the enormous talent that goes with it, have made her a box-office success time after time in films like 'Kramer versus Kramer', 'The French Lieutenant's Woman', and 'Out of Africa' in which she starred beside Robert Redford.

b) Underline any words or phrases which help you to link particular sentences together.

2 Before articles can go into a magazine they are checked by the editor for length and for possible errors. When you have written the first draft of your text, get others in your group to check your script in the same way.

3 You have been asked to give a talk to your class entitled 'The person I most admire'. Write down what you would say. Look at the Summary box below before you begin to write.

SUMMARY BOX

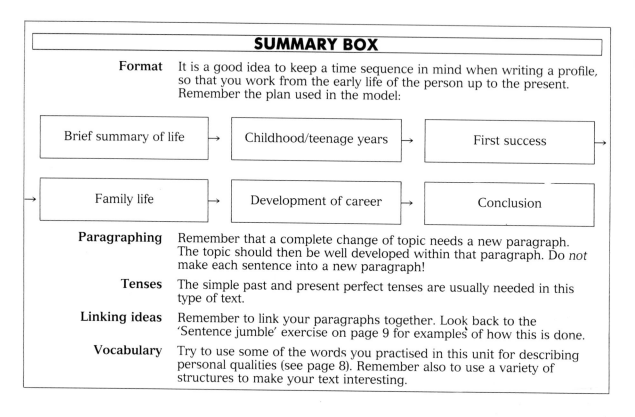

Format It is a good idea to keep a time sequence in mind when writing a profile, so that you work from the early life of the person up to the present. Remember the plan used in the model:

Brief summary of life → Childhood/teenage years → First success →

→ Family life → Development of career → Conclusion

Paragraphing Remember that a complete change of topic needs a new paragraph. The topic should then be well developed within that paragraph. Do *not* make each sentence into a new paragraph!

Tenses The simple past and present perfect tenses are usually needed in this type of text.

Linking ideas Remember to link your paragraphs together. Look back to the 'Sentence jumble' exercise on page 9 for examples of how this is done.

Vocabulary Try to use some of the words you practised in this unit for describing personal qualities (see page 8). Remember also to use a variety of structures to make your text interesting.

Invitations and Refusals

Layout 1 Read the informal letter below, in which the writer is inviting a friend to stay. The letter contains basic mistakes in layout, spelling and punctuation (especially the use of the apostrophe!). Work with your partner to correct the errors, then write out the letter correctly, in three paragraphs.

'Coastguard cottages'
Scotland

sue smith
ebury road 16
victoria
london ec6 1pr

monday 14 september

hello paula!

many thanks for you're letter and apology's for the delay in replying but Ive been up to my eye's preparing for our holiday next week anyway the reason Im writing now is to invite you to a party at our home on new years' eve as you know its jims' birthday on the 1st january so we thought wed make it a double celebration we wondered whether youd like to stay for the whole weekend then we could show you round the city it would be really good to have you here so do try and make it well Id better stop now and get back to the packing I suppose I shall need a holiday just to recover from the preparations love from us both

yours faithfully,

Sue

---

2 With your partner, check that you know the answers to the following:

a) When writing an informal letter in English, where do you normally put your own name?
b) How can you begin and end a friendly letter? How would this be different in a formal letter?
c) 'I'd better stop now' is a typical way to sign off an informal letter. Do you know any similar alternatives? How do you sign off a formal letter?

Functional language

In your corrected version of the model letter, pick out the phrase(s) used for the following:

a) thanking
b) inviting
c) apologising
d) persuading
e) bringing the letter to a conclusion

Can you suggest alternatives for each?

Tenses

Present perfect

> **I've been up to my eyes preparing for our holiday next week.**

1 Can you explain why the present perfect is used in the sentence above?

2 Make questions from the following prompts to interview your neighbour, using the present perfect (simple or continuous) or the past simple.

a) What / you / up to / lately?
b) How much free time / you / have / recently?
c) How long / you / work / your present job?
d) How / you / spend / your time / during / last / few weeks?
e) How / you / spend / last weekend?

Punctuation

Apostrophes

1 Study the use of the apostrophe in the sentences below. Can you work out any rules? Why is there no apostrophe in f)?

a) *She's* gone!
b) *She's* not coming back.
c) *John's* car has been stolen.
d) That *girl's* face is familiar.
e) The policeman took down the *boys'* names.
f) The dog has lost *its* collar.
g) You will find ties in the *men's* department, downstairs.

2 In the following sentences, the apostrophe has been used incorrectly. Can you spot the mistakes? Check your answers with others in your group.

a) Its been a long time since Ive been to Toms' flat.
b) All the boy's wallets had been stolen so they had to walk home.
c) Ive got my umbrella, but have you got your's?
d) We go to a womens' aerobic class on Tuesday's.
e) People are flocking to the aquarium to see the dolphin and it's new baby.
f) Have you seen the dog? Its' got it's lead completely twisted.

Sentence jumble

This is the letter which Paula sent after staying with Sue and Jim for the weekend. Work with your partner to put Paula's letter into the correct order.

Coastguard Cottages,
Dunmore,
Skye,
Scotland

Wednesday, 5th January

Dear Sue,

a)	I think you'd like it up here – the cottage is miles from anywhere so you'd have real peace and quiet.	☐
b)	Living in the country is wonderful but it *is* good to get back to civilisation once in a while.	☐
c)	That punch[1] certainly lived up to its name – no wonder we all had hangovers the next day!	☐
d)	I'm mentioning it now so that you can keep your diary free for that time.	☐
e)	Just a quick line to thank you again for the lovely weekend in London.	☐
f)	Well, that's all for now.	☐
g)	There's plenty of fishing for Jim, too – he can even go shark-fishing if he's feeling ambitious!	☐
h)	Anyway, it certainly got everyone into the party spirit quickly, which is what you want at New Year, after all.	☐
i)	It was such a nice change from my usual surroundings.	☐
j)	Now, what about *you* coming up to see *me* during the Easter holidays?	☐
k)	I hope Jim has recovered from his party by now!	☐
l)	Drop me a line as soon as you can.	☐

Love,
Paula

[1]*punch*: drink made of wine or spirits mixed with sugar, lemons spice, etc.

Format

Paula's letter (above) could be divided into three paragraphs. Write a summary of the three main parts of the letter in the boxes below.

Salutation (*Dear Sue*)	→		→		→		→	Signature

Register

Remember that in letter-writing, as elsewhere, it is important to adapt your language to your audience. Mistakes in style may make your letter look odd or just plain silly!

Some of the phrases below are more formal than others. Tick those you think are suitable for a friend.

- [ ] Thanks for...
- [ ] I am writing to thank you for...
- [ ] My wife and I request the pleasure of your company at...
- [ ] How about coming to...
- [ ] I would like to apologise most sincerely on behalf of...
- [ ] I'm afraid I can't make it to...
- [ ] Apologies for...
- [ ] I'm writing to inform you that...
- [ ] I'm writing to inquire about...
- [ ] I just had to write and tell you about...
- [ ] Must rush now and...
- [ ] Do write soon...
- [ ] I look forward to your prompt reply...

Refusing invitations/ Making excuses

In Britain, if you have to turn down an invitation, it is usual to provide an excuse, otherwise you may appear rude or off-hand, for example:

A: Do you fancy coming to the cinema on Friday?
B: *Oh dear! What a shame. I'm afraid I've got something on that night. What about Sunday?*

1 Can you think of any other ways of refusing an invitation politely?

2 Use the prompts below to invite your partner out. They should turn down your invitation politely, giving an excuse and suggesting an alternative where appropriate.

a) We / have / party / Friday. How / about / come?
b) My parents / rent / cottage / seaside / week. You / like / come / stay / us?
c) Fancy / come / restaurant / tonight? It / my birthday.
d) You / do / anything / weekend? I / think / about / have / few people / over / dinner.
e) How / you / feel / come / holiday / me / this year?

3 Now write a short note inviting someone in your class out for the evening, or away for a weekend. When you are ready, exchange notes (your teacher will deliver them) and write a note refusing the invitation. Remember to give an excuse, and maybe suggest an alternative.

Writing

1 This is the letter which Sue sent to Paula, replying to the invitation to spend Easter in Scotland. Working with your partner, build up the letter from the prompts given.

London
13th January

Dear Paula,

It / be / lovely / hear / you / so / soon. I / be / glad / you / enjoy / weekend / us. We / certainly / love / have / you / here.

I / be / afraid / we / not able / make it / Scotland / Easter. Jim / already / book / us / holiday / Crete / that time / and / it / be / too late / cancel / now. It / be / real shame / as / we / love / come up / otherwise. What about / you / come / here again, though? We / be able / show you / all / things we / not / have / time see / New Year. We / get / three weeks holiday / August / so / that / be / good time, / unless / you / have / other plans / of course. Anyway, / let / me / know / what / you / think / either way.

Have to / rush / now / if / I / be / to / catch / last / post.

Jim / send / love.

Write soon!

Sue

2

> especially as I hadn't seen him for ages!
>   Anyway the real reason I'm writing is to invite you over here in September. I've managed to get time off work for a week – from the 21st to the 28th – so I'll be able to show you the sights and take in some late nights without worrying about work the next morning! Do say you can come – we'd have a great time together!

You have received this invitation from a British friend but unfortunately you have promised to attend a cousin's wedding in your town that very week in September. Write a letter to your friend explaining the situation and suggesting alternative plans. You should lay out your letter correctly and write about 200–250 words, including the following points:

- apologies for any delay in replying (and an excuse!)
- news of yourself/what you have been doing recently
- thanks for the invitation
- polite refusal (and reason)
- alternative suggestions:
  - a) could you change the dates in September?
  - b) could your friend visit you instead?
  - c) would it be best to leave the holiday until Christmas, or the following year?
- 'signing off' phrase
- suitable ending

Look at the Summary box at the end of the unit before you begin writing.

3 You are spending a few months in a foreign country. Write a letter to an English-speaking friend describing where you are and what you have been doing. Include an invitation to your friend to spend a few days with you and suggest how you could spend the time together.

SUMMARY BOX	
Layout	Check with the model letters that you remember how to lay out your letter correctly.
Paragraphing	Group your ideas together into definite topic areas – avoid writing a series of one-sentence paragraphs.
Register	You are writing to friends – make sure your language is not too stiff and formal.
Tenses	Remember that the present perfect (simple or continuous) is useful for describing recent activities.

Giving Personal Information

To start you talking Do students in your country usually take on jobs for the summer holidays? Do/Did you? What is the most unusual or enjoyable job you've done?

Answering advertisements 1 Read the job advertisement below. What sort of qualities do you think they are looking for from prospective candidates?

> **CREW[1] WANTED!**
> **Can you sail? We are looking for active and enthusiastic recruits to crew our sailing vessel 'The Skylark'.**
> 5 **Along with their normal sailing duties, the crew will be working with disadvantaged[2] young people and helping to provide an active programme for them.**
> **Job description and application form from:**
> 10 **Activities Centre**
> **8, Drake Street**
> **London EC1 1PQ**

[1]crew: the people working on a ship
[2]disadvantaged: not having the same opportunities as others

2 Here is one of the letters sent to the Activities Centre, asking for information. Can you spot any mistakes?

activities centre
8 drake street
london EC11PQ

Paul Hunt
Granby Street, 231
birmingham
26 june 1990

dear sir/madam,
I am writing to you about your advertisement in "the times" for crew members for "the skylark". I would be grateful if you sent me a "job description" and the necessary aplication form.

Do write soon.

best wishes

Paul

17

3 Jane Ellis, a nurse, saw the advertisement in the newspaper and decided to write off for further details. Below you can see the information Jane filled in on her application form, but the headings have been removed. Can you supply suitable headings for each entry?

Job application form

Personal

(1) *Full name*   Jane Rachel Ellis

(2) ——————— The Cottage, 2 West Street, Southampton, SW4 2AA

(3) ——————— Southampton 842796

(4) ——————— Totton General Hospital, 26 Staines Road, Totton, Hampshire

(5) ——————— Southampton 842968

(6) ——————— 26th June 1968

(7) ——————— Single

(8) ——————— Excellent

(9) ——————— Photography; member of camera club
Sports; member of local gymnastics, tennis and sailing clubs

(10) *Education*
1973 – 1978   Glenn House Primary, Isleworth, Middlesex
1978 – 1985   West Park Comprehensive, Hounslow, Middlesex

(11) ——————— G.C.E. 'O' levels: Mathematics, English Language, History, French, Spanish, Biology
G.C.E. 'A' levels: English, Human Biology

(12) ———————

Period Covered	:	1988 to present (still employed)
Employer	:	Totton General Hospital
Position	:	Staff Nurse (RGN)

Totton General is a busy modern hospital with 600 beds. At present I am in charge of the intensive care ward, with a staff of eight under my supervision. My responsibilities include dealing with administration, training student nurses, and of course the day to day running of the ward.

(13) ———————

Period Covered	:	1985 – 1988
Employer	:	Malham General Hospital, Yorkshire
Position	:	Nurse

Describing your job

Notice the following useful expressions used on the form:

> At present...
> I am in charge of...
> (I have) a staff of... under my supervision
> My responsibilities include... and the running of the...

1 Look back at the paragraph in which Jane summarises her current responsibilities. Check any problems with your teacher. Then look at the pictures below and write a one paragraph summary for each, using the prompts provided.

a) The Royal / five-star hotel / 300 bedrooms / situated / centre / town. At present / I / charge / catering / have / staff / twelve / my supervision.
My responsibilities / include / make up menus, / purchase / and / course / day-to-day running / kitchen.

b) Kings Park / large, mixed comprehensive / outskirts / town. Present / I / charge / English department / have / six teachers / supervision. Responsibilities / check timetables / teacher-training / and / day-to-day running / department.

2 Write a similar one paragraph summary of your job, or of that of a relative or friend.

Filling in forms

Imagine you work in an employment agency. Interview another person in your class and fill in the application form for him/her.

JOB APPLICATION FORM

Personal:

Full name:

Home address:

Telephone:

Work address:

Telephone:

Date of birth:

Status:

Health:

Interests:

Education:

Qualifications:

Languages:

Present employment:

Previous employment:

Note: Sometimes you are asked to send a *curriculum vitae (CV)* with your letter of application. In a CV, you are expected to supply the same type of information as above, using your own headings.

Read the job description below, which Jane received with her application form.

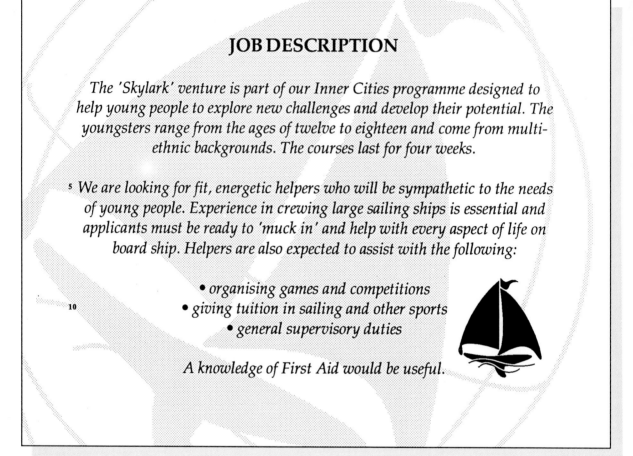

JOB DESCRIPTION

The 'Skylark' venture is part of our Inner Cities programme designed to help young people to explore new challenges and develop their potential. The youngsters range from the ages of twelve to eighteen and come from multi-ethnic backgrounds. The courses last for four weeks.

5 We are looking for fit, energetic helpers who will be sympathetic to the needs of young people. Experience in crewing large sailing ships is essential and applicants must be ready to 'muck in' and help with every aspect of life on board ship. Helpers are also expected to assist with the following:

- *organising games and competitions*
- *giving tuition in sailing and other sports*
- *general supervisory duties*

10

A knowledge of First Aid would be useful.

Vocabulary

Find words or phrases in the text which mean the same as the following:

1 course of action in which result is uncertain
2 young people
3 of different racial groups
4 to help sail a ship
5 aspects of character/abilities which can be developed
6 to join in with the work
7 instruction
8 actions which test the abilities of a person

Discussion

Discuss the following questions:

1 Would this sort of job appeal to you? Why/Why not?

2 Have you ever done a similar sort of job or been a participant on a similar sort of course?

3 Look at the job description again. Do you think the job will suit Jane? Why/Why not?

4 Look back to Jane's application form. Which aspects of her life/ experience should she make the most of in her letter of application?

Letter jumble

1 Here is the letter of application which Jane wrote to send with her form. Working with your partner, put the sentences into a logical order. You may like to photocopy and cut the text into strips to do this exercise.

The Cottage,
2, West Street,
Southampton SW4 2AA

Activities Centre,
Drake Street,
London EC1 1PQ   1st July, 1989

Dear Sir/Madam,

a) As a nurse, I have to be prepared to take on any job in the ward, *no matter* how menial or unpleasant. ☐

b) *During this time* I gained a great deal of experience in dealing with teenagers from all sorts of backgrounds. ☐

c) *Needless to say*, I'd also be happy to be in charge of First Aid and health problems. ☐

d) As my application form shows, I have been a nurse for five years, two of which were spent on a children's ward. ☐

e) I am *also* a member of the Southampton sailing club and have crewed all sorts of ships; I have even sailed to America as one of the crew delivering a yacht to its new owner there. ☐

f) I look forward to hearing from you. ☐

g) *Consequently* I very much hope that my application will be successful. ☐

h) I would *therefore* be quite happy to 'muck in' and tackle any tasks required on the boat. ☐

i) I am writing to apply for the post of crew member on 'The Skylark'. ☐

j) I loved looking after young people and I feel I would have no problems entertaining them, or being firm when necessary! ☐

k) *To sum up*, the post you advertise would give me the break from nursing which I am looking for and would give me the chance to work with young people, which I would really enjoy. ☐

l) *As regards* fitness, I belong to the local gymnastics and tennis club and am a regular participant. ☐

Yours faithfully,

Jane Ellis

---

2 Now group the sentences into five paragraphs and decide on the correct order for the paragraph summaries below.

| 1 | → | 2 | → | 3 | → | 4 | → | 5 |

a) summary of reasons why she is suitable for the post
b) sports/sailing activities
c) reason for writing
d) nursing experience
e) her willingness to 'muck in'

Connectors

In the jumbled letter, the connectors are in *italics*. Look back to check how the following words are used.

needless to say   consequently   no matter   as regards   to sum up

Use one of these to fill each blank below.

1 I have visited many countries; I _____ have useful experience of different cultures and customs.
2 I can swim, ski and sail. _____, I think I have the necessary qualities for the job.
3 _____ qualifications, I have a post-graduate degree from a British university.
4 He was one hour late for the interview. _____, he didn't get the job.
5 _____ how early I get up in the morning, I still can't get to work on time.

Useful language

Complete the following sentences in a logical way.

1 She is very brave; she'll tackle any challenge, *no matter* _____.
2 As a psychologist he has *a great deal of experience in* _____.
3 He's interested in doing all sorts of 'do it yourself' jobs; *these include* _____.
4 This post would give me a chance to travel, *which* _____.
5 *I'd like to sum up* this letter by _____.

Now make up your own sentences using the words in *italics*.

Writing

1 You are looking for a summer job and see this advertisement in the local paper.

COURIERS NEEDED!!

To guide parties of British and American tourists around places of interest in your region.

Applicants should have a good command of English and a pleasant, confident manner.

Write with CV (in English, please!) to our London headquarters:
Intertours,
16 Charles Street,
Balham,
London NE6 1PT

Write a letter of about 250 words in reply to the advertisement. You may like to include some of the following points:

- your work experience, past and present/how your experience fits you for the job
- your character/ability to work with groups of people
- your knowledge of your own countryside/places of interest
- your knowledge of English/other languages

Read the Summary box at the end of this unit before you begin.

CHILDREN'S COURIERS

Looking for a summer job in 1990? Join Eurocamp as a Children's Courier and put your skills to use organising fun and games for children aged 5-14 at one of our campsites in Europe. You'll be working from mid-May to mid-September.

Write to:

Gail Bradshawe, Courier Department, Ref G3, Eurocamp Travel Ltd, Edmundson House, Tatton Street, Knutsford, Cheshire WA16 6BG

Eurocamp

You are interested in the above advertisement and decide to send a CV (*curriculum vitae*) and accompanying letter. Write the letter of application which you will send with your CV. Look at the Summary box below before you begin to write.

3 You are interested in the job advertised here and decide to write for details, enclosing a brief letter of application. Write the letter you would send.

WANTED!
Volunteers for the summer to help run hostels for international groups. Duties include cooking, cleaning and entertaining! Further details from:
**Economy Holidays,
16 Binsey Lane,
Taunton
TX1 32R**

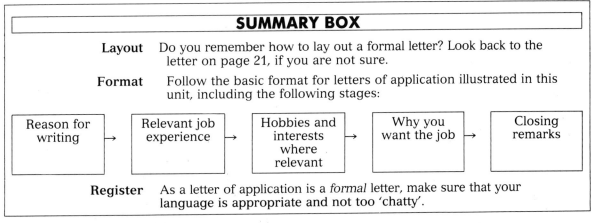

SUMMARY BOX

Layout Do you remember how to lay out a formal letter? Look back to the letter on page 21, if you are not sure.

Format Follow the basic format for letters of application illustrated in this unit, including the following stages:

Reason for writing	→	Relevant job experience	→	Hobbies and interests where relevant	→	Why you want the job	→	Closing remarks

Register As a letter of application is a *formal* letter, make sure that your language is appropriate and not too 'chatty'.

For and Against

To start you thinking

Get into groups to discuss these questions.

1 Have you got a TV in your home? If so, what sort of programmes do you like/dislike watching? Do you only turn on for a programme you particularly want to see or do you leave the television on as a 'background'?

2 Is there too much 'sex and violence' on TV in your opinion? Do you think these kinds of programmes can influence the children and adults who watch them? Give examples.

3 What do families who watch too much TV miss out on? What did people do in the days before the TV became a household object?

Brainstorming

What are the advantages and the disadvantages of owning a TV? Note down as many points as you can think of below. Then compare your ideas with those of your partner. Can you extend the list between you?

Owning a TV — for and against

Advantages	Disadvantages
1	1
2	2
3	3
4	4
5	5

Now read the text on page 25 and find out if the writer covers similar arguments to the ones you have thought of.

Vocabulary

Match the following words which come from the text with their correct definition. Use your dictionary to check your answers.

1 controversy   a) at fault

2 glued to   b) uninteresting

3 to blame   c) person who pays rent to stay in someone's house

4 lodger   d) pattern of behaviour caused by disorder of the mind

5 syndrome   e) (informal) continually close to

6 flop   f) confined to the house e.g. through ill health

7 housebound   g) collapse, sit down heavily

8 blessing   h) strong impression or effect

9 impact   i) a gift from God, something one is glad of

10 banal   j) prolonged argument, especially over social, moral or political matters

TV:
could you be without it?

Ninety-eight per cent of us in Britain have a TV set in our homes and, according to the experts, we rarely turn *it* off. In fact, the average viewer watches as much as 25½ hours a week. Yet television still provokes controversy.

TV does undoubtedly have its bad side. Whilst any links between on and off screen violence have yet to be proved, *few* could deny that seeing too much fictional brutality can desensitise us to real-life horrors.

Furthermore, even when programmes contain neither sex nor violence, it's not really a good thing for so many families to spend whole evenings glued to the box. Some primary school teachers are complaining of youngsters' inability to concentrate and *their* need to be constantly entertained. It would seem that too much TV is to blame.

Of course, it's not only children whose happiness can be affected by television. It can lead to the 'lodger' syndrome, where some husbands come home, flop down in front of the TV and simply don't communicate with *their* families at all. In some homes, soap operas have become a substitute for real life.

Yet there is another side to the picture. For the lonely, elderly or housebound, television can be a blessing, being a cheap and convenient form of entertainment and a 'friendly face' *in the house*. It can be an ideal way to relax, without necessarily turning you into a square-eyed addict.

Television doesn't just entertain, of course. There are times when *it* can be informative and can provide a source of good family conversation. There is no evidence that other hobbies and interests have lost out, either. In fact, it seems that television has helped to popularise some games, like snooker and darts.

And a final point. Over the past few years, television has played a crucial role in disaster relief. During the Ethiopian famine in 1984, the huge fund-raising efforts of Band Aid might have had little impact without the heart-rending pictures we saw on our screens, or the world-wide link up of millions of viewers who donated money to *the cause*.

Informative, useful, entertaining and relaxing – and yes, banal and boring – television is all of these. But if we're not selective, surely we have only ourselves to blame. TV can be part of family life, but when *it* becomes all of *it*, maybe *that's* the time to reach for the 'off' switch. □

Paragraphing

1 Did the first paragraph of the model text make you want to read on? Why/Why not?

2 What is the topic of each of the paragraphs in the model?

3 Do you think the writer gives a balanced view of the pros and cons of TV? Explain why/why not.

4 Does the final paragraph form a good conclusion to the text? Why/Why not?

Linking words

The words in *italics* in the model text help to link the text together. Each refers back to a word used earlier. Find the original word and draw a circle round it.

Format

The text you have just read falls into four basic steps and thus follows a typical format for this type of 'for and against' writing. Work with your partner to complete the basic plan of the text below.

General statement of the problem/ current situation	→		→		→	

Check your answer with the Summary box on page 30.

Listing points

These are the points made for and against TV in the model text. Tick off the ones you noted down yourself at the beginning of the unit.

For TV

1 Can be a blessing for the old and lonely

2 Cheap and convenient

3 Can be an ideal way to relax

4 Can be informative and thought-provoking

5 Has helped to popularise some games

6 Has helped in disaster relief

Against TV

1 Too much violence can desensitise us to real-life horrors

2 Can make children unable to concentrate

3 Children become dependent on laid-on entertainment

4 Can lead to lack of communication in home

5 Can become substitute for real life

Did you think of any different points from the ones in the text? What were they?

Planning

When writing a 'for and against' composition, it is especially important that you make a clear plan before you begin to write. It is a good idea to note down the pros and cons as you think of them, in two separate lists.

Later in this unit you will be asked to write for and against single sex education. To gather some ideas, go round the class and find out:

a) which types of education other members of the class have experienced since starting school – single sex, coeducation or both.
b) what most people preferred/would have preferred, and why.

Now, from the information you have collected, note down at least three pros and cons of single-sex education.

Writing first paragraphs

1 Look at the following opening paragraphs of four different 'for and against' texts and, with your partner, decide which are the most/least interesting. Can you say why?

A
'Working mothers mean neglected children'. No doubt a sizeable section of the population would like to rise up and lynch the gentleman who made this claim the other day. Yet there are many, too, who would agree with him. So who is right – the mother who chooses (or is forced) to go out to earn a living or the one who stays at home?

B
There are two sides to every question. This applies to the necessity for military service as well as everything else.

C
Package holidays can be a good idea but it depends. Let us look at the pros and cons of the situation.

D
'Speak roughly to your little child. And beat him when he sneezes . . .'. This verse comes from the children's book 'Alice in Wonderland' and is, of course, not intended to be taken seriously. But the question of how we should discipline our children is very much in the news. It is now against the law in Britain for a teacher to smack a child in school and it is suggested that the same law should be extended to parents. So what *are* the rights and wrongs of smacking your child?

2 It is extremely important to make your opening paragraph interesting. You may want to give some surprising facts or statistics, to make a controversial statement or even to begin with a quotation – the important thing is to persuade your reader that you have something interesting to say.

Write suitable opening paragraphs on the following 'for and against' topics. You have been given help with the first one, which you should write out in full. When you have finished the second one, exchange papers with your neighbour. Does their opening paragraph make you want to read on?

a) Frozen embryos, genetic engineering . . . Are scientists going too far?

Scientists / make / amazing advances / past few decades. Test tube babies / become / familiar phenomenon / and / techniques / store / frozen embryos / future use / evolve. Genetic engineering / soon / give / means / control / make-up / offspring.

Yet / question / arise: / 'We / go / too / far?'

b) Single-sex schools – are they good for our children?

Linking contradictory facts

> *Whilst* any links between on and off screen violence have yet to be proved, few could deny that seeing too much fictional brutality can desensitise us to real life horrors.

We often want to mention both sides of the question in one sentence, as in the example above. Other words used to make contrasting points are:

although   yet   however   nevertheless   in spite of   on the other hand

1 Rework the example sentence, using each of the words in the box above.

2 Now work with your partner to complete the following sentences.

a) Travelling by air is still one of the safest ways to travel, in spite of _____

b) It seems terrible that we should use animals for experiments. Yet _____

c) Nuclear power would seem to be the answer to the world's fuel crisis. On the other hand _____

d) In Britain the number of women who smoke is increasing despite _____

e) Whilst genetic engineering opens exciting prospects for scientists _____

Making your text 'flow'

Connectors

A 'for and against' composition should not just consist of a list of ideas. Sentences need to be linked by suitable words (*Firstly, Moreover, In conclusion,* etc.). Ideas within individual sentences need to be moulded too, and the correct and varied use of connectors is important in giving your writing style.

In the text below, the writer is outlining the disadvantages of a career in acting. First read Text A, which is really just a list of points. Then use connectors to improve the style of the text (B) by choosing suitable words to fill the blanks.

Text A

> You should realise that acting is a risky career. Every year thousands of young hopefuls leave drama school. Few achieve the fame and glamour they seek. It is a fact that anyone who does make it into an acting company has got to be prepared for hard work and unsociable hours. Many companies expect you to rehearse all day but also to 'give your all' on stage in the evening. No place here for the lazy. It is a fact that much of an actor's life is spent touring. You will have to be prepared for uncomfortable nights in cheap boarding-houses. Most actors spend a lot of time 'resting' (that is, waiting for employment). They have to be prepared to take on extremely menial jobs just to make ends meet. A career in acting should only be considered by those with energy, enthusiasm, resilience – and, of course, talent!

Text B

(1) _____, you should realise that acting is a risky career. Every year, thousands of young hopefuls leave drama school (2) _____ few achieve the fame and glamour they seek. (3) _____, it is a fact that anyone who does make it into an acting company has got to be prepared for hard work and unsociable hours; (4) _____ many companies expect you (5) _____ to rehearse all day but also to 'give your all' on stage in the evening. No place here for the lazy. It is (6) _____ a fact that much of an actor's life is spent touring, (7) _____ you will have to be prepared for uncomfortable nights in cheap boarding houses. (8) _____ most actors spend a lot of time 'resting' (that is, waiting for employment), they have to be prepared to take on extremely menial jobs just to make ends meet. (9) _____, a career in acting should only be considered by those with energy, enthusiasm, resilience – and, of course, talent!

1 a) At first   b) To begin with   c) At the beginning
2 a) yet   b) only   c) except
3 a) Secondly   b) As well   c) Moreover
4 a) so   b) in fact   c) as
5 a) not only   b) in addition   c) furthermore
6 a) in addition   b) too   c) also
7 a) as a result   b) therefore   c) so
8 a) Due to   b) Besides   c) Since
9 a) Finally   b) To sum up   c) In total

Writing

1 Text jumble

Here is a 'for and against' text about using animals for experiments. Working with your partner, put the sentences into a logical order. You may like to copy and cut the text into strips to do this exercise.

a)	This is because drugs which are tested and found safe for animals can have a completely different effect on humans.	☐
b)	And, finally, when animals suffer purely for our fashion and beauty industries, surely this is the time to draw the line.	☐
c)	The elimination of polio and the discovery of penicillin each depended on animal testing and there was no satisfactory alternative.	☐
d)	Bombs have been placed in fur departments of shops and food contaminated with poisons before it leaves the factory.	☐
e)	To begin with, over 90,000 animals die every week in British laboratories, yet many researchers admit that experiments can be ineffective.	☐
f)	Secondly, it must always be remembered that if drugs weren't tested on animals first, children could die as a result of taking untested drugs.	☐
g)	This would surely be an indefensible situation.	☐
h)	However this medical use needs to be strictly limited and alternative techniques – like cell-culture – should be used whenever possible.	☐
i)	Yet although we may violently disapprove of such actions, have Animal Rights groups got a valid point to make?	☐
j)	All in all, it would seem that the use of animals in experiments is essential in promoting medical advances.	☐
k)	People in Britain have been shocked by the acts of terrorism carried out by Animal Liberation groups over the past few years.	☐
l)	First of all, it is a fact that the major discoveries in medicine have come from experiments on animals.	☐
m)	There is another side to the question, however.	☐

Now group your text into at least four clear paragraphs.

2 Write an article of about 300 words for the class magazine on the topic 'Single-sex schools – are they good for our children?' Use the paragraph you wrote in the 'Writing first paragraphs' exercise on page 27 as your introduction. Read the Summary box at the end of this unit before you begin to write.

3 Write an article of about 300 words in answer to *one* of the questions below, outlining both sides of the question.

a) Medical advances – are doctors and scientists going too far?
b) Is life better now than it was 100 years ago?

Read the Summary box below before you begin to write.

SUMMARY BOX

Planning	Remember to make a clear plan before you start writing. Jot down your ideas in two separate columns, pros and cons. If you find you're short of ideas, go and ask your family and friends for their opinions!
Paragraphing	Make sure you have at least four paragraphs, as in the format below:

General statement of the problem/ current situation	→	Points for	→	Points against	→	Conclusion/ weighing up the points outlined and coming to some decision

Try to make your opening paragraph interesting and original in the ways outlined earlier in this unit.

Answering the question	Remember that you are asked to give arguments for *and* against the topic you have chosen. Try to give equal weight to both, if possible, and make sure that your final decision is a well-balanced consideration of the points you have outlined.
Linking ideas	Remember to use suitable connectors to link the points in your argument, e.g. *firstly, to begin with, secondly, moreover, besides, furthermore, all in all, finally.*

Can you remember how to link contradictory facts in your argument?

Notes and Messages

Short notes

Look at the notes and messages below and decide with your partner what you would say if you were actually speaking to the person. What sort of words do you need to supply?

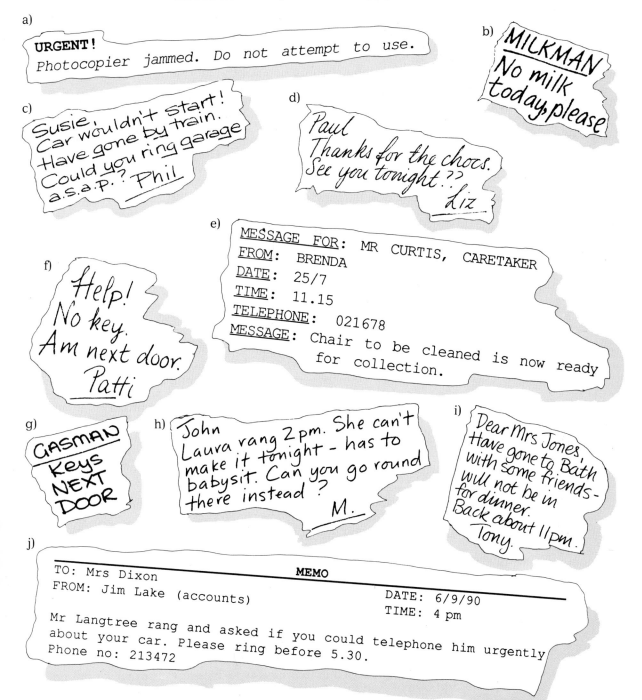

a)

URGENT!
Photocopier jammed. Do not attempt to use.

b)

MILKMAN
No milk today, please

c)

Susie,
Car wouldn't start!
Have gone by train.
Could you ring garage
a.s.a.p.? Phil

d)

Paul
Thanks for the chocs.
See you tonight??
Liz

e)

MESSAGE FOR: MR CURTIS, CARETAKER
FROM: BRENDA
DATE: 25/7
TIME: 11.15
TELEPHONE: 021678
MESSAGE: Chair to be cleaned is now ready for collection.

f)

Help!
No key.
Am next door.
Patti

g)

GASMAN
Keys
NEXT
DOOR

h)

John
Laura rang 2 pm. She can't make it tonight - has to babysit. Can you go round there instead?
M.

i)

Dear Mrs Jones,
Have gone to Bath with some friends - will not be in for dinner. Back about 11 pm.
Tony.

j)

MEMO
TO: Mrs Dixon
FROM: Jim Lake (accounts)
DATE: 6/9/90
TIME: 4 pm

Mr Langtree rang and asked if you could telephone him urgently about your car. Please ring before 5.30.
Phone no: 213472

Being brief

The following messages are too long. With a partner, shorten them to approximately the number of words given in brackets, by deleting unnecessary words. Then write your version in the appropriate boxes. You may use abbreviations where appropriate. For example:

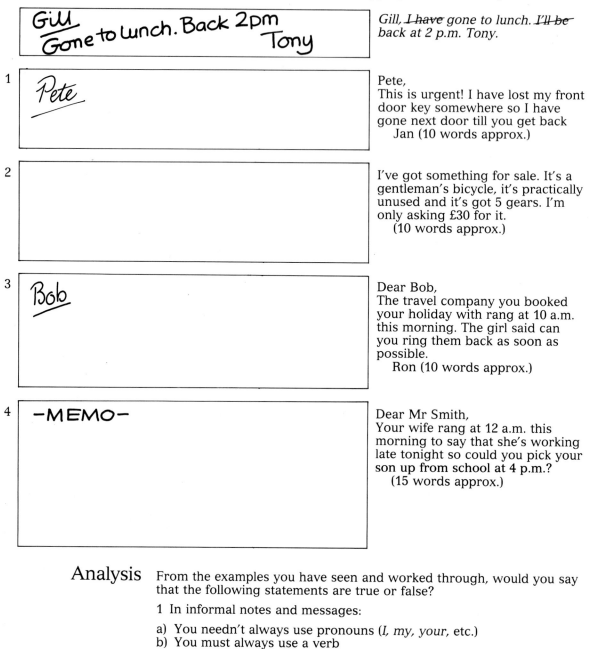

Gill
Gone to lunch. Back 2pm
Tony

Gill, ~~I have~~ gone to lunch. ~~I'll be~~ back at 2 p.m. Tony.

1 *Pete*

Pete,
This is urgent! I have lost my front door key somewhere so I have gone next door till you get back
Jan (10 words approx.)

2

I've got something for sale. It's a gentleman's bicycle, it's practically unused and it's got 5 gears. I'm only asking £30 for it.
(10 words approx.)

3 *Bob*

Dear Bob,
The travel company you booked your holiday with rang at 10 a.m. this morning. The girl said can you ring them back as soon as possible.
Ron (10 words approx.)

4 —MEMO—

Dear Mr Smith,
Your wife rang at 12 a.m. this morning to say that she's working late tonight so could you pick your son up from school at 4 p.m.?
(15 words approx.)

Analysis

From the examples you have seen and worked through, would you say that the following statements are true or false?

1 In informal notes and messages:

a) You needn't always use pronouns (*I, my, your,* etc.)
b) You must always use a verb
c) You can use abbreviations (*a.m., a.s.a.p., phone no.*)
d) Definite articles (*a, the*) can be left out
e) It isn't always necessary to write complete sentences
f) You should always use connectors (*and, so, because,* etc.)

2 There is no difference between messages to friends and the sort of messages you write at work.

3 The language used in 'business-type' messages is usually more polite and formal than that used in messages to friends.

Abbreviations

Abbreviations are often used in notes and messages. Check that you know what each of the following mean. If you are not sure, look in an English-English dictionary such as the *Longman Dictionary of Contemporary English.*

1 info.	6 N.B.	11 PTO	16 encl.
2 &	7 IOU	12 s.a.e.	17 St.
3 re.	8 max.	13 i.e.	18 Rd.
4 etc.	9 a.s.a.p.	14 c/o	19 doz.
5 v. imp.	10 no.	15 incl.	20 P.O.

Writing notes

Work with a partner to write notes/messages for the following situations:

1 Write a note to someone in your class, suggesting a date for this evening. State where/when, etc. Your teacher will deliver them. Write a note to accept or refuse with a good excuse when you receive a note yourself.

2 You've lost your watch while staying in a country cottage in Scotland. Write a note for the next tenants, asking them to send it on to you if they find it.

3 You've broken the alarm clock in your room while on a holiday in England. Write a note for your landlady, explaining what's happened and what you're doing about it.

Detailed notes: information sheets

Sometimes we need to write rather longer notes than those illustrated at the beginning of this unit. More detailed notes contain the same basic features as we have already seen (abbreviated sentences, omission of pronouns, articles, etc.).

In the notes below, the owner of a seaside cottage has left information for a holiday tenant about the cottage. Read through the text with your partner, and think about the sort of words which would be needed to make complete sentences. Then do the Comprehension Check exercise below.

Keys Key with copper wire - front door. Similar key back door. Third key for cellar door down steps outside back door - contains wood & coal for fires.
Window locks Kitchen windows will be locked when you arrive & need to be re-locked when you leave (insurance regulations). Key is in drawer near fridge.
5 **Immersion heater** operates on night storage & will be on when you arrive - please turn off before you go. If you need more hot water there is a booster system which takes an hour. Instructions for use will be on chest of drawers beside heater cupboard in front right-hand bedroom.
Storage heaters operate on night storage. 2 in living room and 1 in kitchen. 1
10 or 2 will be on according to the weather. (If it's really warm switch them off!)
Dustbins collected Friday morning. Rubbish in plastic sack to be put out late Thursday eve on roadside at top of path leading down to cottage. Any rubbish you leave after this will be taken by caretaker. Plastic sacks in cupboard
15 under sink.
Fridge/Freezer will be on when you arrive - please switch off before you leave.

There are basic essentials e.g. salt, pepper, T-bags, t.rolls, washing-up liquid etc. in the cottage. You are welcome to use them but please replace or leave a note of
20 anything that you use the last of. The shop in the Cove is open 6-7 pm in summer & the 2 shops in Ruan Minor even later. All also open on Sundays in the season.

Comprehension

The following notes come from the model text. Can you build them into complete sentences by completing the blanks? You may need to supply articles (*a, the*), verbs (*is, are*), pronouns, or even complete phrases, for example:

____ Key with ____ copper wire ____ ____ ____ front door.
The key with *the* copper wire *is for the* front door.

1 ____ Third key ____ for ____ cellar door, ____ ____ down ____ steps outside ____ back door.

2 (HEATER) ____ Instructions will be on ____ chest of drawers beside ____ heater cupboard in ____ bedroom.

3 ____ Key is in ____ drawer near ____ fridge.

4 Dustbins ____ collected ____ Friday mornings.

5 ____ Rubbish in ____ plastic sack ____ to be put out late ____ Thursday evening on ____ roadside at ____ top of ____ path leading down to ____ cottage.

6 ____ ____ Plastic sacks in ____ cupboard under ____ sink.

Format

Detailed notes need to be clear, precise and easy to read. It is often useful to divide them into topic areas, under separate headings, as in the model.

Notice that the writer takes care to be polite when leaving orders: *Please* switch off..., *Please* don't bother her, etc.

Tenses

Passive forms

> **Photocopier jammed**
> **Chair to be cleaned now ready for collection**

In notes we are often more interested in the action itself than in the person performing the action. The use of the passive can also give a neutral, formal style to a note or message. Complete the following using the passive.

1 You'll need to relock the windows before you leave.
The windows _____
2 The former tenants should have unplugged the heater.
The heater _____
3 You are to put out the rubbish every night.
The rubbish _____
4 You'll have to tip the caretaker.
The caretaker _____
5 Probably nobody will have watered the garden.
The garden _____

Detailed notes: Giving directions

The owner of the cottage also sent some directions to her tenant, explaining how to find the way to the place. Read the directions (on page 35) aloud to your partner, filling in the missing words.

Can you say which form of the verb is used for giving directions?

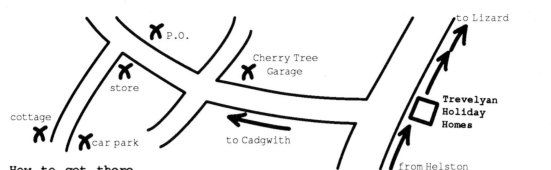

How to get there

Watch out for sign for Trevelyan Holiday Homes, on R, about 3 mls from Lizard. Signpost indicates left-hand turning marked Cadgwith/Ruan Minor. Drive until you come to the Cherry Tree Garage & go straight over crossroads (do not take right-hand turn to Cadgwith
5 marked 'Heavy Vehicles Route'). Go through Ruan village, past church & P.O. then take left turn at general store. Go down steep very narrow lane & Tregwyn is the first thatched cottage on the right at the bottom. Opp. on the left is a space marked 'Private Car Park'. Do not put car too far forward on fire hydrant or
10 flowers (will explain this later).

Writing

1 Write notes or messages for the following situations:

a) An English-speaking friend is coming round to see you this evening but you've been asked to go and babysit at short notice. Leave a message for your friend telling her where you are and inviting her to go round.

b) You're on a language course in Britain but one day you are ill and can't attend school. Write a note for the teacher which a friend can take for you.

c) You work for a British company. Your boss is out when someone calls to make an appointment for the secretarial job advertised in the paper. Write a memo for your boss, telling him what arrangements you have made.

d) The TV isn't working. You've phoned the repair man and he's coming this afternoon while you're out. Leave a note for your English-speaking flatmate, asking her to stay in for his call.

2 While you are away on holiday, some English-speaking friends are coming to stay in your house. Write the notes you would leave. Remember that these are just notes so you do *not* need to write whole sentences. Also, they are for a friend, so they needn't be too formal – but they must be clear! The following suggestions may help you to decide on the sections of your notes:

- Do your friends need instructions on using equipment, e.g. the dishwasher, washing machine, cooker, microwave? Remember to use the polite imperative (*Please switch off...*).
- Does anything need doing in the garden?
  Have you left any pets? If so, what do they need?
- Is there a milkman, newspaper boy, etc. to be paid?
- What are the arrangements for paying gas, electricity, the telephone?
- What is there to do/see in the area? How is it best to get about?
- What other information might be of use to them?

Look at the Summary box at the end of the unit before you begin to write.

3 With a partner, write down some directions which you could send to an English-speaking visitor to your school. She will be travelling from the centre of town by car, on foot or by public transport (you decide which). You should write your directions in note form, as in the model text, but make sure they are clear. Start by sketching a map of the route. You may find the following language useful:

Bear left/right
Watch out for...
Take the left/right-hand turn/
  turning into (Grange Road)
It's the first/second, etc. on the
  right
Drive until you come to...
Go straight on as far as...
Go straight over the crossroads/
  roundabout
Go down the road/lane
Look for signs to...
Look for a road marked...

Go on past/over/across...
a crossroads
a T-junction
a subway
a pedestrian crossing
a turning
a slip road
a roundabout
a side street

SUMMARY BOX

Style
Remember that when writing notes we frequently leave out pronouns, articles, prepositions, and occasionally verbs. We can also use abbreviations.

Notes must always be clear and unambiguous. Do not shorten a note/ message so much that the meaning is lost. As a check, give your note to a friend and see if the meaning is plain to them.

Register
A message to a friend will probably look different – and sound different – from a note to the boss. Always keep in mind the audience you are writing for.

Detailed notes
Long notes need to be clearly laid out. Remember to group different topics in sections, with a clear heading for each.

Writing a Formal Letter of Complaint

To start you thinking

1 How often have you been abroad on holiday? Where? When? With whom?

2 What has been a) your best and b) your worst holiday till now? Describe them in detail.

3 Have you ever written a letter to complain about a holiday? If so, what was the result?

A letter of complaint

Now read the model letter on page 38 and underline the words/phrases the writer uses for complaining.

Revision: layout

Quickly check with your partner that you can answer the following questions:

1 Where should you write your own address in an English letter?

2 Would you normally include your name with the address?

3 In what kind of letter should you write the name and address of the recipient? Where?

4 Can you remember how to begin and end a formal letter? How does this differ when you know the name of the recipient?

5 How would you begin and end a letter to a close friend?

Paragraphing

It is important to write well-planned and fully developed paragraphs in any type of formal text. (Take care not to write each sentence on a new line.) Most paragraphs contain one topic sentence, often at the beginning, but sometimes elsewhere in the paragraph. Can you pick out the topic sentence in the example below?

The plane was late and we had to spend six hours in the airport lounge with no refreshments. When we finally got on the plane we had to wait yet another forty minutes for flight clearance, without a single word of apology from the pilot. And when we got to our destination there was nobody to meet us and we had to find our own way to the hotel by public transport. As an example of how *not* to organise a holiday, this trip could have won a prize!

What is the topic of each of the paragraphs in the model letter on page 38? Can you pick out the key sentence in paragraphs 2 and 3? Do the other sentences in each of these paragraphs contribute to the key sentence? Make a list of all the words and phrases you can find which:

a) link the sentences in each paragraph
b) link the paragraphs together

16 Stratton Road,
Throop,
Bournemouth,
Dorset BP9 3HQ

Bedford Tours,
118 Eastcliff Road,
Bournemouth,
Dorset BQ8 4NZ

27th April, 1990

Dear Sir/Madam,

My family and I have just returned from one of your
'weekend breaks' in Paris (April 23-26) and I am writing
to express my strong dissatisfaction at the holiday we
were given.

5   To begin with, the hotel was not at all as we had been
led to expect from your brochure. As the bar was open to
non-residents, the foyer was permanently noisy and
dirty. In fact, the noise from the disco was so bad that
getting to sleep before 2 am on any night was virtually
10 impossible. The bedrooms, too, were not up to standard:
in our room, the walls were damp, the basin was cracked
and the windows were caked with grime[1] and did not open.
As for my daughter's bedroom, the heating did not work
and the bed had not been changed since the last
15 occupant.
     Added to all this, the 'fully-trained and experienced
courier' we had been promised turned out to be a
university student on a vacation job. Mr Johnson's hold
on the French language[2] was, to say the least, tenuous[3]
20 and one of our party had to step in and act as
interpreter on many occasions. Not only did Mr Johnson
have problems on this score[4] but he was obviously
totally unfamiliar with our route. This was evident on
the second day when he turned up, late, for our coach
25 trip around the capital, examining a large map. When we
got going, it became clear that he was having great
difficulty in following this map and we consequently
spent much of our day kneeling on our seats peering out
of the back window of the coach at the places we had
30 just missed!
     As you will realise, we are thoroughly disgusted with
the holiday your company provided. I trust you will
agree that at the very least we deserve a letter of
explanation from you and a substantial refund of our
35 money. Unless this is forthcoming, we shall have to take
matters a step further.

Yours faithfully,

M C Clark

(Mr M C Clark)

[1]*caked with grime*: covered
with a coating of dirt
[2]*his hold on the language*:
his knowledge of the
language
[3]*tenuous*: uncertain
[4]*on this score*: as far as
this was concerned

Format

The letter from Mr Clark falls into four basic steps. Work with your partner to complete the basic plan of the text below:

Reason for writing/place and date of holiday	→		→		→	

Useful language

Tick off the complaint language which you have already underlined in the model letter.

- ☐ I am writing to express my strong dissatisfaction at...
- ☐ I am writing to complain about...
- ☐ We were extremely disappointed with...
- ☐ ...was not what we had been led to expect
- ☐ The...was so bad that...
- ☐ It was not up to standard
- ☐ It didn't work/was out of use
- ☐ We were appalled to find...
- ☐ We were thoroughly disgusted with...
- ☐ We expect (a letter of explanation / a substantial refund)
- ☐ Unless..., we shall take matters further
- ☐ I should warn you that...

Register

When Mr Clark was telling his neighbour about his holiday he used very direct language. Look in the model text to find formal equivalents of these words and phrases:

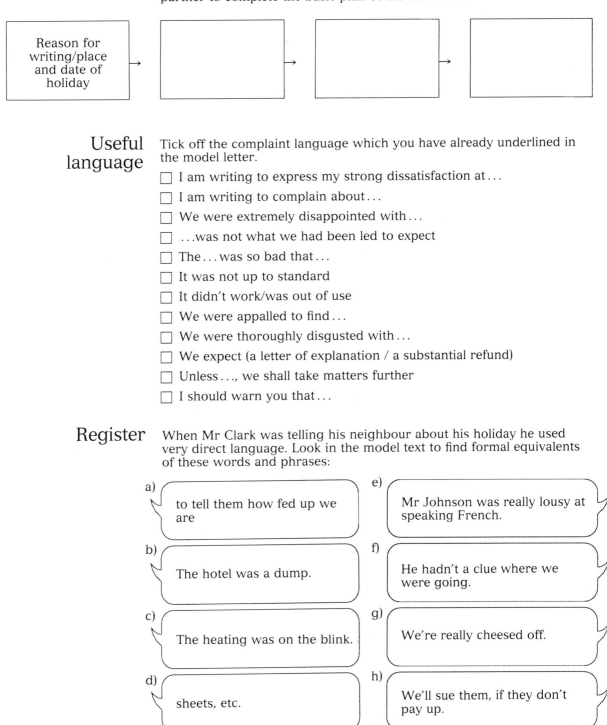

a) to tell them how fed up we are

b) The hotel was a dump.

c) The heating was on the blink.

d) sheets, etc.

e) Mr Johnson was really lousy at speaking French.

f) He hadn't a clue where we were going.

g) We're really cheesed off.

h) We'll sue them, if they don't pay up.

Register is obviously extremely important in letters. In a formal letter, be careful not to use colloquial words or expressions which are out of keeping with the tone of the text.

Linking words

In the exercise on 'Paragraphing' (page 37) you looked at how sentences/paragraphs can be linked. Now, work with your partner to choose the best word or phrase to fill the blanks in the following text. More than one answer may sometimes be possible.

Dear Mr Temple,

I have just had my house decorated by your company and I am writing to complain about the totally unsatisfactory standard of work done.

(1) _____ , (2) _____ I had originally arranged for work to begin on the 1st of this month, nobody turned up (3) _____ , (4) _____ , the wrong date had been entered in your diary. (5) _____ I was forced to take another day's leave (6) _____ be at home when the painters arrived. (7) _____ my holiday entitlement is limited to only three weeks a year, I could (8) _____ little afford to do this.

(9) _____ , had anything like a decent job been performed by your men, I would have had no more to say about this. (10) _____ , this was not the case. I was, (11) _____ , appalled when I arrived home to find such a shoddy job done. The wallpaper, (12) _____ , was already peeling off the walls in places and was (13) _____ quite noticeably ripped in two places. (14) _____ , the paintwork had (15) _____ not been sanded down and the new paint was cracked and blotchy. (16) _____ , cupboard doors had been painted closed and were (17) _____ impossible to open once the paint had dried. (18) _____ I had to use a chisel to prize them open again.

I telephoned your company first thing yesterday about this matter and they promised you would ring me back before 1 p.m. (19) _____ this assurance, I have heard nothing and I should warn you that (20) _____ I do so in the very near future I intend to take the matter further. (21) _____ I already have an appointment with my solicitor for this Friday.

I look forward to your prompt reply,

D. Smith

---

1 a) First of all   b) In the beginning   c) At the beginning
   d) To start with
2 a) in spite of   b) despite   c) although   d) even
3 a) although   b) though   c) thus   d) as
4 a) seemingly   b) however   c) nevertheless   d) apparently
5 a) So   b) Consequently   c) And   d) Thus
6 a) so as   b) for to   c) so as to   d) in order to
7 a) Because   b) As   c) Although   d) Considering
8 a) nevertheless   b) thus   c) obviously   d) indeed
9 a) Nonetheless   b) Frankly   c) However   d) But
10 a) Indeed   b) Unfortunately   c) Conversely   d) On the other hand
11 a) therefore,   b) thus   c) frankly   d) in fact
12 a) actually   b) for instance   c) for example   d) on the one hand
13 a) too   b) also   c) moreover   d) furthermore
14 a) Secondly,   b) Added to this,   c) Next,   d) Not only
15 a) clearly   b) obviously   c) evidently   d) hardly
16 a) On the other hand   b) To make matters worse   c) Furthermore
   d) And
17 a) for that reason   b) hardly   c) therefore   d) consequently
18 a) At least   b) At last   c) At the end   d) In the end
19 a) Despite of   b) Although   c) In spite of   d) Notwithstanding
20 a) except   b) without   c) until   d) unless
21 a) Indeed   b) Thus   c) For that   d) In fact

Text correction

Work with your partner to find mistakes in the letter of complaint below. (These include grammar, punctuation, vocabulary, paragraphing and layout.)

Nicole Flury   Bournemouth 19th January 1990

                                Blarney Hotel
                                Cork

Dear Sir,

I am writing to inform you of my gross dissatisfaction with your hotel, where I have just spent 10 days. It was an absolute nightmare. For the sunshine you guaranteed we waited in vain, it rained non-stop. The staff was surly, moved as
5 slow as a snile and worked frightful. As if this wasn't enough the food left much to be desired, the portions were microscopic and wouldn't have satisfied a mouse. The "heated outdoor swimming pool" was stone cold and paradise of flora and fauna so nobody was particularly fond of taking the bath.
10 The only thing which left was playing golf and tennis, fishing and horseriding but because of the bad weather conditions it wasn't possible to enjoy it.

I hope you take this letter seriously and change these bad conditions or at least the brochure.

15 Yours faithfully

Nicole Flury

Nicole Flury

Brainstorming

What sort of things can spoil a holiday? Make a list. The pictures below may help you.

Writing

1 You have just returned from a two-week package holiday which was a disaster from start to finish. Write a letter of about 250 words to the travel company outlining what went wrong and stating what you expect the company to do about it. You may like to use the plan given below to help you. Look at the Summary box at the end of this unit before you begin to write.

Introduction : Reason for writing. Exact details of holiday (time, place, etc.)

Development : Details of problems. You may need to deal with each major problem in a new paragraph.

Conclusion : What you expect from the company.

2 You have just spent a month at the school advertised below and were not at all satisfied with several aspects of your stay. Write a letter to the director of the school giving reasons for your dissatisfaction, based on the notes you have made and encircled. Look at the Summary box at the end of this unit before you begin to write.

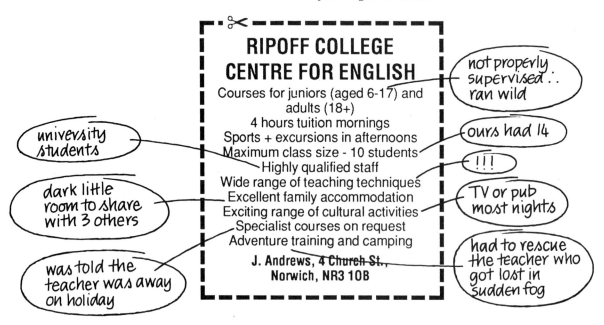

3 You ordered a music system some weeks ago and when it finally arrived, after a long delay, you discovered it did not work properly. Although the firm has sent repairmen out to you on two occasions you are still not satisfied. Write a letter of about 250 words to the manager of the firm explaining what has happened and saying what you want him to do next.

SUMMARY BOX	
Layout	Check with the model letter that you remember how to lay out a formal letter correctly.
Paragraphing	Group your ideas into definite topic areas. Make sure you back statements with plenty of examples/illustrations. Try to link your paragraphs with suitable connectors, e.g. *to begin with, added to all this*, etc.
Register	You are writing a formal letter – make sure your language is not too direct!

Describing Appearances

Text correction

1 Look at the description below, which was written by a student. With your partner, see how many mistakes you can find in grammar, vocabulary and style.

2 Look at the way the student has divided the text into paragraphs. How do you think these paragraphs could be improved?

Four years ago I began work in a sport shop to win a bit of money. Every Saturdays I was anxious because I wasn't an expert on this field. Soon one of the managers of the shop accosted me. I was worried that he has been angry with me but in fact he was very helpful. Today I can say that I know him very well and that he is probably my best friend. His name is Jean-Pierre.

The first thing that impressed me was his moustaches. I have always been impressed by moustaches because they make serious. He is a tall, thin, Swiss man in his early twenty's. He has green eyes and his skin is always sunburned. On his free time, he is used to practising sport: every kind of sport and he's an expert on every discipline. He is used to wearing fashionable shirts and trousers. Nevertheless he likes to be dressed in blue jeans.

Although he is very reliable at his work, he's a pleasant boy who we can speak and laugh. He has an incomparable sense of humour but he needs to have a big friendship to prove it. He is a shy, down-to-earth man but he isn't always very well in his skin. Jean-Pierre isn't really an adventurous man although the quality to make us enjoy them too.

I hope to keep this particular friendship until my death.

Format

In spite of the errors, the student obviously made a basic plan of the text before beginning to write. What is the format? Complete the boxes below.

| Introduction/ How they met | → | | → | | → | |

Making a description vivid

Physical descriptions often occur as thumbnail sketches in a piece of writing rather than as an extended composition. Read the three descriptions below. Why do you think they are so effective? Is it because:

a) adjectives are well-chosen?
b) adjectives are often used in an original way?
c) the description is divided into short, manageable sentences?
d) the writer keeps his feelings out of the description?
e) any other reasons?

> Mr Boggis strode briskly up the drive. He was a small, fat-legged man with a belly. His face was round and rosy and two large brown eyes bulged out at you. He was dressed in a black suit with a dog-collar round his neck and on his head a soft black hat. He carried an old oak walking stick which lent him, in his opinion, a rather rustic, easy-going air.
>
> *(Roald Dahl)*

> At the appointed time, Mr Roydon was shown in to my library and I got up to meet him. He was a small neat man with a slightly ginger goatee beard. He wore a black velvet jacket, a rust-brown tie, a red pullover and black suede shoes. I shook his small, neat hand.
>
> *(Roald Dahl)*

> She had been only five feet tall even before she became bent from age and toil. Her broad strong face is deeply lined and she has taken on the wispy, papery look of the old. But she is, nevertheless, commanding. Her blue eyes are steady, authoritative but kind. Her hands and feet are large, knobbly, with big joints – the hands and feet of an old working person who has scrubbed many a floor.
>
> *(Reader's Digest)*

Descriptive adjectives

Notice how many descriptive adjectives the writers use in each of the texts. Good descriptions often contain a wide range of adjectives and adverbs, although it is quality rather than quantity which counts. One adjective used in an original and imaginative way can be more effective than a list of everyday ones.

1 Make a list of the adjectives used in the three texts above and check that you understand them.

2 Work with your partner to put the following adjectives into three columns: **Size, Personality, Physical appearance.** Put a tick (✓) by those which are definitely positive and a cross (✗) by those which are definitely negative. Use your dictionary to help you, when necessary.

> bubbly plump astute mousy slender balding freckled huge easy-going tiny bouncy skinny spotty tallish chubby short-sighted bossy pasty round-shouldered pushy bright tattooed mischievous minute tousled

Are there any which are used more frequently for women than for men (and *vice versa?*)

Describing appearances

Clothes

1 Identify the following in the picture on the next page:

a) curls
b) a lace collar
c) a frock
d) socks

e) laces
f) wellington boots
g) track suit bottoms
h) trainers

i) a fringe
j) puff sleeves
k) a crew cut

2 Can you guess what material the clothes are made of? Choose from the list below, for example:

a *cotton* dress

canvas	silk	nylon	leather	fur	velvet
suede	plastic	cotton	acrylic	wool	rubber

Can you add any more materials to the list?

Physical appearance

How observant are you? Close your eyes and describe your teacher to the person sitting next to you. They will correct you if you get things wrong. When you have finished, get your partner to close their eyes and describe one other member of the class whom you have chosen.

General physical descriptions

1 Look at the paragraph below, in which the writer describes her first meeting with one of the children in the photo above. Which child do you think she is describing? Work with your partner to fill the blanks – you may need more than one word to do this. Try and make your description as vivid as possible!

I opened the door and there stood the most (1) _____ boy
I could have imagined. He was wearing a (2) _____ ,
(3) _____ shirt, already (4) _____ and
(5) _____ (we soon found out that nothing stayed
(6) _____ on Michael), (7) _____ ,
(8) _____ trousers and (9) _____ trainers.
His (10) _____ hair was cut (11) _____ in a
crewcut which gave him rather the appearance of
(12) _____ . But it was his eyes which really caught my
attention. They were (13) _____ , (14) _____
and full of (15) _____ . I realised life was going to be
(16) _____ but (17) _____ with this
(18) _____ member of the household.

---

2 Look at the other children in the photo. What sort of personalities do you think they have? Tell your partner.

3 Now imagine that one of the other children in the photograph has come to stay in your house for a few days while their mother is in hospital. Write a paragraph similar to the one above. Include details of where you first met, what they were wearing, general physical appearance and character. When you have finished, compare your text with your partner's. Which one is the most vivid? Why?

Describing personal qualities

1 What sort of person would your ideal partner be? Choose eight adjectives from the list and number them according to their importance to you. Discuss your choice with your neighbour. Do their answers surprise you?

even-tempered	sensitive	witty	ambitious	self-reliant	
dependable	good fun	passionate	loyal	down-to-earth	creative
impulsive	self-confident	generous	easy-going	caring	intelligent

2 Can you think of any more words you would like to add to your own list?

3 What sort of person would you hate your partner to become? Make a similar list of eight personal adjectives (e.g. *bossy, selfish,* etc).

Choosing the right word

Adjective, adverb or noun?
Fill the gaps in the sentences with the correct form of the words in the box (you may need to use the negative form).

decisive	lazy	impatient	strong	assertive
confident	beautiful	resolute	ambitious	elegant

1 She was a clever woman but she lacked _____ and never took the trouble to put herself forward for promotion.

2 He stretched out _____ on the sand, enjoying the stillness of the afternoon.

3 The woman was _____ dressed in a twin-set and pearls.

4 People who find it hard to stand up for their rights need training in _____.

5 He was a little over- _____ of his abilities and was shocked to find his boss had demoted him.

6 She was one of the great _____ of that decade.

7 They tried to persuade her not to marry him, but she was absolutely _____.

8 He was respected for his _____ of character.

9 Despite his _____ he was a kind man.

10 William was certainly easy-going but, being rather _____ by nature, he could never bring himself to give a firm opinion on any course of action.

Order of adjectives

Put the following in the correct order. Can you work out a rule for the position of adjectives?

1 Tom was a little/rather aggressive/fat/child.
2 She had blue/enormous/bright/eyes.
3 Her hair was a mass of red/long/curls.
4 He was wearing a leather/black/very pricey/jacket.
5 On her head she had a(n) black/little/feather/amazing/hat.
6 He was wearing tight/velvet/trendy trousers.
7 He was carrying a(n) walking/old/lovely stick.

Now check your answers with the 'Order of adjectives' diagram on page 48.

Discussion

Look at the pictures below and discuss the following questions with your neighbour.

1 What does the person look like? What are they wearing?
2 What are they doing in the picture?
3 What sort of person do you imagine they are? Why?
4 How are they feeling now? Why?
5 What are they doing in this place?
6 What else can you say about them?

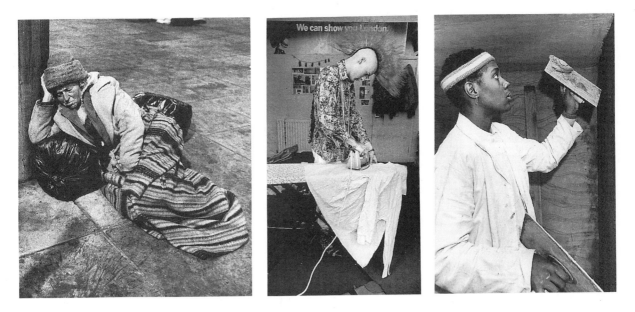

Writing

1 a) Use the prompts given to write a paragraph describing the girl in the picture.

When / I / first / meet / Karen / she / sit / verandah / motel / bottle / lemonade / front / her. / She / outstandingly attractive / woman / mid-twenties / blond / wispy hair. She / wear / rather elegant / blue / silk / dress, / sleeveless / with / low back / short skirt. / Spite / obvious youth / she / look / tired / defeated. As / I / approach / she / look / up / and / give / me / small smile / welcome.

They were/looked/
appeared/seemed...
They were wearing/
dressed in...
in their teens/middle-
aged/elderly
in their early-/mid-/
late-thirties
They were short-
sighted/round-
shouldered/
well-dressed

b) Write a paragraph of about 80 words describing your first meeting with *one* of the people in the photos on page 47. Begin your paragraph with the words: 'When I first met....

2 Write a paragraph describing your first meeting with a boyfriend/ girlfriend/best friend. Use the description in question 1 as a model. Before you begin to write, look at the Summary box at the end of this unit. The 'useful language' will also help you.

3 Write a description in about 300 words of an interesting person you met once. (It could be a pop-singer, an actor, a TV personality, etc).

SUMMARY BOX

Format   Remember to set out your description in clear paragraphs as in the plan below:

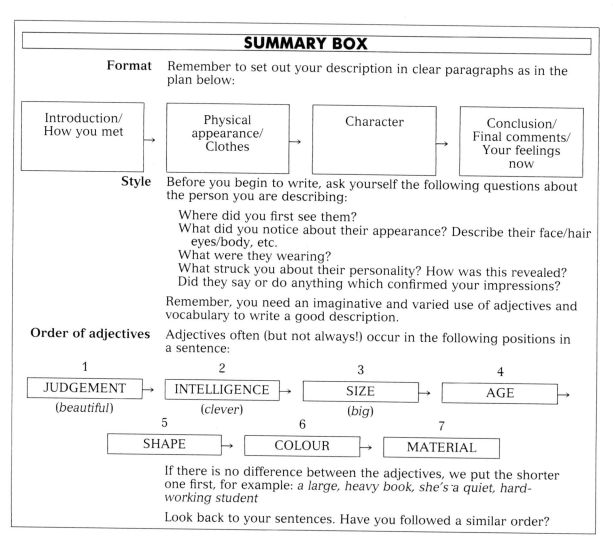

| Introduction/ How you met | → | Physical appearance/ Clothes | → | Character | → | Conclusion/ Final comments/ Your feelings now |

Style   Before you begin to write, ask yourself the following questions about the person you are describing:

    Where did you first see them?
    What did you notice about their appearance? Describe their face/hair
      eyes/body, etc.
    What were they wearing?
    What struck you about their personality? How was this revealed?
    Did they say or do anything which confirmed your impressions?

Remember, you need an imaginative and varied use of adjectives and vocabulary to write a good description.

Order of adjectives   Adjectives often (but not always!) occur in the following positions in a sentence:

| 1 JUDGEMENT *(beautiful)* | → | 2 INTELLIGENCE *(clever)* | → | 3 SIZE *(big)* | → | 4 AGE | → |

| 5 SHAPE | → | 6 COLOUR | → | 7 MATERIAL |

If there is no difference between the adjectives, we put the shorter one first, for example: *a large, heavy book, she's a quiet, hard-working student*

Look back to your sentences. Have you followed a similar order?

Advertisements and Notices

Newspaper announcements

Answer the following questions in groups.

1 Read through these advertisements and announcements which come from a newspaper and decide which column they come from. Choose from the list below.

Holidays	Births	Birthdays
Obituaries	Accommodation to let	Entertainments
Articles for sale	Personal	Engagements
Lost and found	Forthcoming events	Property for sale

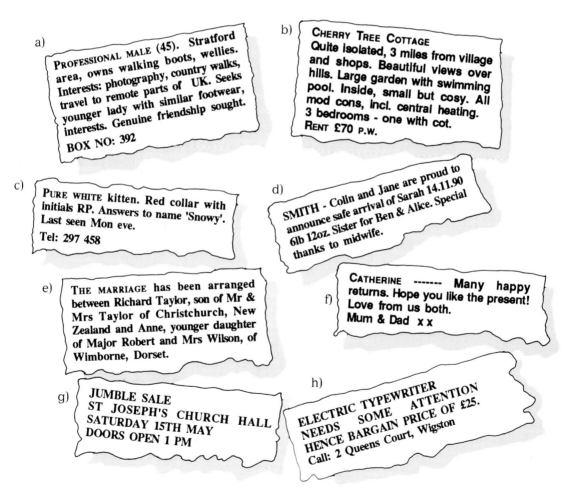

a) PROFESSIONAL MALE (45). Stratford area, owns walking boots, wellies. Interests: photography, country walks, travel to remote parts of UK. Seeks younger lady with similar footwear, interests. Genuine friendship sought.
BOX NO: 392

b) CHERRY TREE COTTAGE Quite isolated, 3 miles from village and shops. Beautiful views over hills. Large garden with swimming pool. Inside, small but cosy. All mod cons, incl. central heating. 3 bedrooms - one with cot.
RENT £70 P.W.

c) PURE WHITE kitten. Red collar with initials RP. Answers to name 'Snowy'. Last seen Mon eve.
Tel: 297 458

d) SMITH - Colin and Jane are proud to announce safe arrival of Sarah 14.11.90 6lb 12oz. Sister for Ben & Alice. Special thanks to midwife.

e) THE MARRIAGE has been arranged between Richard Taylor, son of Mr & Mrs Taylor of Christchurch, New Zealand and Anne, younger daughter of Major Robert and Mrs Wilson, of Wimborne, Dorset.

f) CATHERINE ------- Many happy returns. Hope you like the present! Love from us both.
Mum & Dad x x

g) JUMBLE SALE ST JOSEPH'S CHURCH HALL SATURDAY 15TH MAY DOORS OPEN 1 PM

h) ELECTRIC TYPEWRITER NEEDS SOME ATTENTION HENCE BARGAIN PRICE OF £25. Call: 2 Queens Court, Wigston

Abbreviations

Advertisements often involve the use of abbreviations. These can be quite specialised, as in the area of property and accommodation. Do you know what is meant by the following? Work in pairs and, when you have finished, check your answers with another pair.

1 mod cons.	7 furn.	13 grnd flr flat
2 incl.	8 h & c	14 spac. kit.
3 c/h	9 d. glazed	15 det. house
4 p.w.	10 lux.	16 mod. bath.
5 eves.	11 tel.	17 attrac. gdns.
6 Box no.	12 mins.	18 g.f. cloaks.

Format

1 What, in your opinion, are the two most important considerations to bear in mind when writing an advertisement for a newspaper?

2 Look again at the advertisements and announcements on page 49. Which of the following have sometimes been omitted? Find examples of each.

a) pronouns (*I, my, he, his*, etc.)
b) articles (*a, the*)
c) verbs
d) prepositions
e) whole phrases
f) connectors (*and, but*, etc.)

3 Look at announcement c) on page 49. It has not been abbreviated in any way. Why?

What to leave out

Read the full description below of a hotel, and then look at how it was shortened for a newspaper advertisement. The writer had to pay for every word printed, so naturally he removed as many unnecessary words as possible.

Queen's Lynn Hotel   ~~This is a~~ traditional 16th century village inn ~~with~~ 11 en-suite bedrooms including ~~a~~ 4-poster. ~~It's also got~~ log fires ~~and~~ full central heating. ~~It's got a~~ reputation for fine food and wine. ~~The sea is only~~ 20 minutes ~~away~~. ~~You can get~~ weekend breaks from £30 per night. Queen's Lynn, Summerton, Norfolk. Telephone (068) 72174.

Working in pairs, decide which words you could leave out when writing advertisements for the following. Remember that the text must remain clear to the reader.

---

1 Isle of Jura, Scotland. We have a comfortable holiday bungalow to let. It sleeps 6 and has a lovely large living room and a fully equipped kitchen. It really is ideally situated for birdwatching, fishing and walking. There are sandy beaches within easy reach of the bungalow. Apply to: Mrs Florence, Argyll Street, Jura. Telephone number (063) 6831.

---

2 **FOR SALE**
I have a ticket for the 'Rolling Stones' concert at the Albert Hall on Monday November 26th. You'll have an excellent seat in the stalls. I only want £20 for the ticket. I've also got a train ticket for London which is available at a reduced price.
Contact: John Fisher, Cypress Road, Fishguard.
Telephone number (026) 75891.

Making sense of advertisements

Fill in the missing words in this advertisement to make complete sentences, for example:

Quite isolated, 3 miles from village and shops
The cottage is quite isolated and is three miles from the village and shops.

> CHERRY TREE COTTAGE
> **Quite isolated, 3 miles from village and shops. Beautiful views over hills. Large garden with swimming pool. Inside, small but cosy. All mod cons, incl. central heating. 3 bedrooms - one with cot.**
> RENT £70 P.W.

Working in groups, practise reading aloud the other advertisements on page 49, in the same way.

Rephrasing information

> **We can help you with your cleaning, washing, ironing, etc.**
> **Help *offered* with housework.**

1 Sometimes it is easiest to rephrase information for the sake of brevity. What do you notice about the verb form in the second sentence? Can you say why it is used here?

2 Shorten the following by rephrasing them in the style of an advertisement, as in the example above. Then discuss your ideas with others in your group. Try to agree on the best version.

a) We're looking for someone who can dance to join our troupe.
   D _____

b) We have houses, bungalows and flats for sale.
   A _____

c) I want someone to share my flat.
   F _____

d) I have lost the money, cash cards and photographs which were in my wallet.
   C _____

e) We want musicians, comedians, magicians, etc. for our Christmas show.
   E _____

Practice

Imagine you want to put an advertisement in the paper for someone to share your flat/house.

1 In groups, decide what you want to say in your advertisement. (What is your flat like? Where is it? What is the rent, and what does that include? What sort of person do you want (and *not* want!)? Will they have their own bedroom? Smoker or non-smoker? etc.)

2 Write down a summary of the points you have decided.

3 Now write an advertisement for the newspaper.

When you have finished, write your version of the advertisement on the classroom board. Which of the advertised flats would *you* choose? Why?

HELP US TO SAVE THE RAINFORESTS

ECOLOGY CLUB
BRING AND BUY SALE

We are holding a bring-and-buy sale to raise funds for our tropical rainforest campaign.

5 The destruction of the environment is possibly the biggest threat to mankind this century. In the ecology club we 10 work to raise public consciousness about the dangers we face. We are in constant need of funds to back our 15 projects — the bring-and-buy sale is just the first of many similar

fund-raising efforts. New members are always needed — why not make this the occasion to come and meet the group and maybe even join us?

20 *PLACE* — St Mary's Church Hall, Winchester
TIME — 7 pm - 9 pm

We need:
• articles, new or secondhand, for sale on the day
• refreshments — sandwiches, cakes, cans of soft drink, etc.
25 • helpers! To work on the stalls and to tidy up later

HELPERS
Anyone willing to help in any capacity is invited to attend a preliminary meeting at 7 pm on June 7th in St Mary's Hall. If you are not able to attend this meeting, but would still like to help, contact:
30 Mr T Watkins, 16 Shirley Drive, Winchester, Tel. 0276 5431.

Note: One of the most important things about an information sheet is that it should be clear and easy to read. Important details like place and time should be highlighted by careful spacing or by clear headings.

Writing your own notice

Get into groups to do the next exercise. You are thinking of starting up a 'Theatre Club' for English-speaking people in your area and have decided to put up a notice in the local library. As a group, make a list of the information you need to include, for example:

- Will you need costumes/scenery, etc. (or people willing to make them)?
- Will you need electricians, stagehands, musicians, or any other experts?
- Will you need actors (with experience or without), directors, make-up artists or others?
- What information can you give about the club and its aims and objectives?
- Where and when will you meet?
- Are you having a preliminary meeting? For whom? Where and when will it be? In case of problems, who should be contacted?

When you have decided on the information to include in your notice, delegate individual members of your group to work on different sections of the notice. If you have an artist, they could even do some illustrations! When everyone is ready, put the pieces together to make one notice, checking for errors or discrepancies.

Writing

1 Use the information below to write an advertisement for a local newspaper. Your advert should be as brief as possible.

> **Personal**
> We are a semi-professional band and we need a male singer to join us. He must be able to sing in a variety of styles – reggae, jazz, pop, etc. We'll be playing at all types of functions on the south coast. The new singer should be aged between 28 and 36. There will be auditions next week.
> Telephone Sue: (896) 0572

When you have written your advertisement, get together with other members of your group and compare your version with theirs. Then as a group, write a final version containing the best of all your efforts.

2 Write advertisements for the following:

a) You are looking for a penfriend. Write an advertisement for the 'Personal' column of an international magazine describing yourself/ your interests.
b) You have lost something valuable. Write an advert for the 'Lost and found' column of an English-speaking newspaper.
c) You want to sell your car. Write an advert for the newspaper describing the car (condition, mileage, reasons for selling it, etc.).

When you have finished, put your advertisement on the class noticeboard/wall. Are the adverts clear? Are they concise?

3 *Either*
a) You are thinking of organising a trip abroad and have decided to put up a notice in your school/place of work to see how much interest there would be in your plans. Write out your notice in about 200 words.

Or
b) You have heard of an emergency appeal from a well-known body (e.g. Red Cross, Greenpeace, etc.) and plan to organise a fund-raising event. Write a notice outlining what you hope to do, and why, and calling for volunteers.

SUMMARY BOX	

Format	Remember that when you place an advertisement in a newspaper you pay for every word, so it is important to write as concisely as possible. You can omit pronouns, articles, verbs, prepositions – even whole verb phrases! However, while it is important to find the shortest way to say something, it is equally important to ensure that the meaning remains clear.
	Remember that notices and information sheets should be set out clearly, with information divided into well defined sections so that it is easy to read. Notices should also be 'eye-catching' – slogans are often useful here, together with some kind of picture/sketch.
Rephrasing information	This is sometimes the best way of limiting the number of words you use while not losing the clarity of your writing. Look back to the exercise on page 51 to remind yourself of this technique.
Abbreviations	These are very commonly used in adverts/notices. You will find lists of common abbreviations in an English-English dictionary such as the *Longman Dictionary of Contemporary English*.

Writing a Letter of Advice

To start you thinking

Discuss the following questions in groups.

1 Do you ever read the 'Problem page' in magazines? Why do you think they are so popular? Would you ever write to a magazine?

2 What sort of language is used to give advice in English? (e.g. *If I were you, I'd...*) Make a list of useful words/phrases.

A letter of advice

The extract below comes from a letter written by an eighteen-year-old to an elder sister. Imagine you were the recipient. What advice would you give? Discuss your ideas with your partner.

> I don't think I can stand being at home any longer. Everything I do is wrong – my clothes, my hair, my friends, everything! You'd think I was still a 10-year-old, the way they treat me. Can you believe I still have to be in at 10 o'clock at night?? Anyway, Sean thinks we should get married and get a house of our own. He says I don't need to stay at school any longer – in fact he'd like us to start a family straight away. What do you think, Rachel? After all, we <u>have</u> been going out for two years now,

Now read the letter of reply on the next page and underline the language used to give advice.

Format

1 Which paragraph of the letter:

a) warns against a course of action? ☐

b) contains an invitation? ☐

c) contains a request? ☐

d) suggests a course of action? ☐

e) refers to some previous correspondence? ☐

Do you agree with the advice? Why/Why not?

16 Stratton Road,
Roath Park,
Cardiff CR9 3PD

Sunday 16th October

Dear Gill,

Thanks for your letter and for the photos- you certainly seem to have had a wonderful holiday. School trips weren't like that in my day!

Well Gill, I'm sorry to hear that you've been having problems at home but I do think you ought to consider very carefully before doing anything as dramatic as rushing into marriage. I know you and Sean have been going out together for 2 years but you're still only eighteen, after all. You'll be giving up ever such a lot if you decide to settle down now. No more parties, discos, holidays - and lots of worries about the kids, the mortgage and making ends meet. And is it a good idea to throw away your chances of getting into university and going into a career you would really like? I'm really glad I did all my training before I got married - and I'm sure you would be too, in the end.

If I were you, I'd have another go at talking to Mum and Dad. Try and tell them calmly how miserable you feel. I could have a word too, if you think that would help. I'm sure they'd be willing to compromise if they really understood the situation. After all, you've only got one more year at home to get through, remember!

Anyway, do take time to think things over, Gill - and don't let Sean talk you into anything you're not absolutely sure about. Why not pop up here to see us next half-term, then we could have a really good chat about the situation? We'd love to see you, you know - and the children would be thrilled.

Well, I think that's all for now. Don't forget to ring or write and tell me how things are going will you? I'll be waiting to hear from you.

Mark and the kids send their love,
Rachel

[1]*mortgage*: money borrowed to buy a house/flat
[2]*making ends meet*: managing financially
[3]*compromise*: take a middle course, acceptable to both sides

2 The model letter contains five main paragraphs. Complete the basic plan of the text in the boxes below:

| Reference to previous correspondence/Reason for writing | → |

| | → | | → | | → |

→ | Standard closure, e.g. *Do write soon!/Looking forward to hearing from you*, etc. |

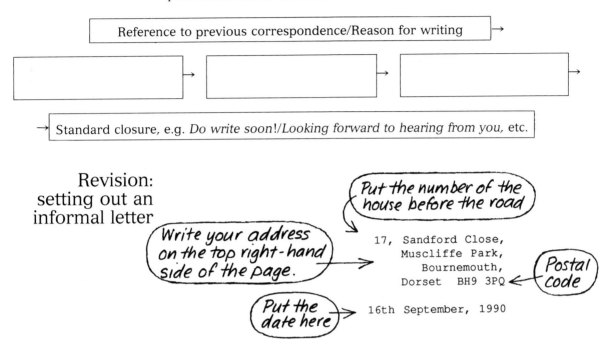

Revision: setting out an informal letter

Write your address on the top right-hand side of the page.

Put the number of the house before the road

17, Sandford Close,
Muscliffe Park,
Bournemouth,
Dorset   BH9 3PQ

Postal code

Put the date here → 16th September, 1990

Note: Remember that you *do not put your name* at the top of the page.

1 In which two of the following do the beginnings *not* match the endings?

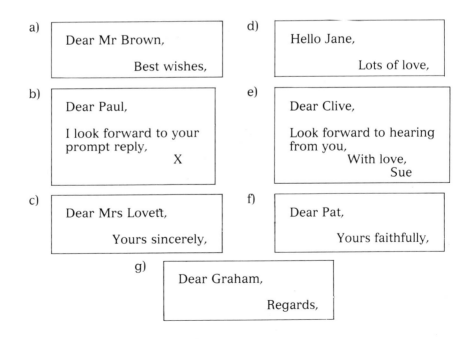

a)

| Dear Mr Brown,

                    Best wishes, |

d)

| Hello Jane,

                    Lots of love, |

b)

| Dear Paul,

I look forward to your
prompt reply,
                    X |

e)

| Dear Clive,

Look forward to hearing
from you,
                    With love,
                    Sue |

c)

| Dear Mrs Lovett,

          Yours sincerely, |

f)

| Dear Pat,

          Yours faithfully, |

g)

| Dear Graham,

               Regards, |

2 Which could be used in a friendly/informal letter?

Language of advice

Tick off the advice language which you listed at the beginning of this unit or which you underlined in the model letter.

- ☐ I really think you ought to...
- ☐ You might consider...
- ☐ How about...?
- ☐ Your best idea would be to...
- ☐ Do/Don't...
- ☐ It might be a good idea to...
- ☐ Have you thought about...?
- ☐ Why not...?
- ☐ My advice would be to...
- ☐ Whatever you do, don't...
- ☐ You could/should...

Phrasal/ Prepositional verbs

Notice how the following verbs are used in the letter, then use an appropriate form in each of the sentences below.

let down	make up for	go out	give up
settle down	fit out	get through	think over

1 I had a terrible headache when I got up – in fact I don't know how I _____ the day.

2 When John got back from holiday, he found his office had been _____ with a new carpet and some nice cupboards.

3 Sally says she's sorry to _____ you _____ but she won't be able to make the appointment today.

4 _____ what I said and give me a ring if you change your mind about the deal.

5 Nothing could ever _____ his loss but in time his family came to accept it.

6 Nigel and Susan have been _____ for five years now but I don't think they plan to get married.

7 Anita regrets _____ working as she's finding it hard to make ends meet.

8 I don't think Andrew will ever _____ ; he loves the wandering life too much.

Punctuation

1 Here is a reply from the 'Problem page' of a magazine. Working with your partner, write out this text again in two paragraphs, using the correct punctuation.

i feel that sixteen is far too young for you to think about marriage even if you feel you are very mature for your age i would strongly advise you not to rush things but to give yourself time before taking such an important decision you are likely have a much better relationship if you allow yourself to mature if you and david are willing to be just good friends for the time being your parents might feel differently about your seeing him if they don't dislike him as a person perhaps you could say to them that the age difference won't seem as important when you are older if on the other hand they have something against him apart from his age you should discuss that too and listen to their point of view

2 When you have finished, underline the advice language in the text.

3 With your partner, discuss what you think the original letter to the magazine said. Do you agree with the advice given?

Writing

1 Read this problem letter to a magazine. In groups, discuss the advice you would give to Yasmin, and then write a letter of reply. Compare your letter with other groups.

■ SHOULD I OBEY MY HEART? ■

Should true love come before family duty? I am a student, aged 19, studying fashion design in London. My parents have always been very 5 strict about friends and expect to choose my husband for me. It is a custom and tradition of our country and I am expected to obey. But I have met and fallen in love with 10 an Italian waiter. I really want to marry him although he is poor, but I will have to choose between my parents and my boyfriend. I can happily live with no money 15 but I can't bear the thought of the hurt it will cause my parents.

There is really no way they can agree to the match so should I give him up? Or should I go my 20 own way and marry him? I feel so unhappy and I can't discuss the problem with my family for obvious reasons. What do you think I should do?

Yasmin

---

2 Get into groups to do the next exercise. You have a problem, real or imaginary, e.g. a problem with a boyfriend/girlfriend, a problem with parents or family, etc. Write a letter to an English magazine, in a similar style to the letter above. When you have finished, exchange your letter with another group and write a suitable reply to the letter you have received. Remember to use advice language from the exercise on page 58. Write only the body of the letter, as in the models. Look at the Summary box at the end of the unit before you begin to write. You may also find the problem language given useful.

3 A friend of yours is fed up with his job and wants to be an air steward. Unfortunately his English is terrible and he must improve it very quickly if he is to succeed at his interview in four months' time. He has written to ask you for advice. How would you reply? Set out your letter in full, including the address (about 250 words). Look at the Summary box at the end of the unit before you begin to write.

SUMMARY BOX

Layout Remember that your address should go at the top right-hand corner of your letter. Do *not* write your name here. In an informal letter, it is not usual to write the address of the recipient. Remember the standard phrases used to open and close a letter (see page 57).

Format Informal letters often follow this basic plan:

> Reference to previous correspondence/Reason for writing →

> Development (divided into paragraphs as necessary) →   Concluding paragraph →

> → Standard closure, e.g. *Do write soon!/Looking forward to hearing from you*, etc.

Advice language Try to vary the language you use for giving advice – use the phrases you have seen/practised in this unit.

Writing a Film or Book Review

To start you thinking

Work in groups to discuss the following questions.

1 What's the best film you've seen in the last year or two? What was it like? Who was in it?

2 Are there certain types of film you would never go and see? What are they?

3 Have you read any good books in English lately? If so, what were they? What were they about? Would you recommend them?

Pre-reading

In the text opposite, film critic Sean French reviews 'Mississippi Burning'. The film deals with the disappearance and subsequent murder of three young men by the Ku Klux Klan. Before you read the text:

1 Use a dictionary if necessary to find out the meanings of these words:

bribery   a riddle   slyly   culprits   gripping

2 Look at the riddle in lines 29/30 of the text. Can you explain the pun? What is the writer trying to suggest about the inhabitants of Mississippi?

3 Find out how much your partner has heard about the Black Civil Rights movement in the US and the Ku Klux Klan.

Comprehension

Work in pairs to decide whether the following questions are true or false:

1 The three young men who disappeared were engaged in the struggle for equal rights for Blacks.

2 J.Edgar Hoover was keen to open an investigation into the disappearances.

3 The FBI paid for information about the murders.

4 According to the film, Mississippi is a strange, dark, uncivilised state.

5 Ward wants to follow normal procedures of investigation.

6 Parker portrays the FBI investigation in a rather unoriginal way.

Paragraphing

Which paragraph in the review:

1 considers the visual aspect of the film?

2 contains an overall criticism (positive and negative) of the way the theme is treated?

3 describes how the film detectives tackle the case?

4 gives us the results of the real-life investigation?

5 explains why the script appealed to the director?

6 describes how the real-life investigation began?

FIRE IN THE HEART OF A SOUTHERN STATE

IN 1964 THREE young men, two white and one black, were driving around Mississippi trying
₅ to persuade local black people to vote. One night they disappeared. The case caused a sensation and the Attorney General,
₁₀ Robert Kennedy, forced the head of the FBI, J. Edgar Hoover, to send a team of officers down south.

₁₅ After six weeks of investigation and a little bribery, they found the bodies and discovered the truth. The young men had been arrested by Mississippi police,
₂₀ handed over to a local branch of the Ku Klux Klan and murdered.

The film is directed by Alan Parker. What clearly fascinated him about the story of 'Mississippi Burning' was that it concerned
₂₅ a strange, dark, uncivilised state in modern America. At the beginning of the film, two FBI agents, Anderson and Ward, are driving south to investigate the disappearance. Anderson poses a riddle: What has four
₃₀ eyes but cannot see? The answer is Mississippi.

Ward is determined to conduct his investigation by the book. Anderson is a Southerner and understands that normal
₃₅ procedure does not apply down there. The Whites are silent and the Blacks scared to talk. Ward's attempts at interrogation continually run up against a brick wall[1] while Anderson slyly wins the confidence of local
₄₀ Whites. Gradually he convinces Ward that only by breaking the rules can the culprits be brought to justice.

Alan Parker is far more interested in images than words and 'Mississippi Burning'
₄₅ is an extraordinary visual experience. His version of the South is a strange, hellish world of fire, decay and darkness, and the evil of racism is conveyed, perhaps too crudely, by the fleshy ugliness of the actors
₅₀ and extras he has chosen to play the white Southerners.

The film has been intensely controversial in America. Parker has represented the Mississippi Blacks as entirely passive
₅₅ victims who can only be saved by white men from the north. He has also created his own version of the FBI investigation, turning it into standard cop drama. Fortunately, Parker has the services of Gene Hackman,
₆₀ in my view the finest screen actor in America, who conveys so much dignity and pain in the face of wickedness that he virtually saves the film single-handedly. 'Mississippi Burning' will cause bitter disagreement, but
₆₅ it will grip virtually everyone who sees it.

[1]*run up against a brick wall*: meet no success

Format

The model review contains four basic steps:

a) Recommendation
b) Plot
c) General comments
d) Introduction/Background to the story

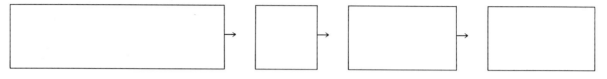

In the boxes above, write the steps in the order in which they occur in the text.

Tenses

1 In the first two paragraphs the writer paints the background to the film. Which tenses does he use? Give examples.

2 Which tenses are used to describe the plot of the film? Why?

Talk to your partner about a good TV drama you have watched in the last few weeks. Describe the plot, using the appropriate tense.

3 Which tenses are used in the final paragraph? Why? Give examples.

Note: The writer of this text moves from Past → Present → Future, which is often a good plan for this type of composition.

Beginning your review

Film, book or TV

1 The model review begins by giving the real-life background to the film. Look at the examples below of other ways in which writers begin their reviews, whether of films, books or TV. Read through them quickly and put them into the correct category.

ON THE FACE of it there are many reasons for not seeing *Pelle the Conqueror*. It's nearly three hours long with a plot that is almost unremittingly[1] depressing, about a middle-aged unemployed labourer at the turn of the century who emigrates with his young son from Sweden to bleak[2] Denmark, of all places. Yet this is one of the most beautiful and enthralling films I've seen this year.

Marie Claire — May 1989

Tim Sebastian looks set to rival John Le Carré with the publication of his new spy thriller, **Spy Shadow** (Simon & Schuster, £11.95).

LAST night's British dramatic offering, **Somewhere to Run** (ITV), was nowhere near so entertaining. It dealt with the fashionable subjects of child abuse and runaway children and was about as gripping[3] as a bald tyre...

Daily Mail — July 1989

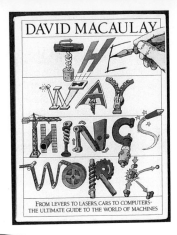

DAVID MACAULAY

THE WAY THINGS WORK

FROM LEVERS TO LASERS, CARS TO COMPUTERS·
THE ULTIMATE GUIDE TO THE WORLD OF MACHINES

WHEN I couldn't operate the space-age radio in my new car recently, the salesman suggested I ask my 11-year-old daughter to explain it to me: 'Kids understand all these things better than we do.' He was right. Which is why I think a new book called **The Way Things Work** by David Macaulay (*Dorling Kindersley*, £15) is not for children but for adults like me, and is going to save me from being patronised[5] by the young for many years to come.

Inside Rose's Kingdom by Matthew Kneale (Gollancz, £11.95) is a macabre[4] tale about a woman who seeks to trap young people, brainwash them and alienate them from their friends and families...

Good Housekeeping — June 1989

'I liked the show too, so what on earth are we going to write about it?'

[1] *unremittingly*: unceasingly, without pause
[2] *bleak*: cold and cheerless
[3] *gripping*: intensely interesting
[4] *macabre*: gruesome, frightful
[5] *patronised*: treated as an inferior

2 Which of the reviews:

a) is ruthlessly critical?
b) relies on the excitement of the plot to raise your interest?
c) seeks to interest you because of its sense of humour?
d) tries to impress by drawing parallels with another writer?
e) tries to surprise you by its contradictory statement?

Do you think all the opening paragraphs are effective? Why/Why not? Which one appeals to you most? Why?

3 Now, write a similar short opening paragraph for a film, book or TV programme you have seen recently. Compare your paragraph with others in your group.

Vocabulary

Work with your partner to put the following words into the appropriate category: **Book, Play, Film.** Some will go into more than one category.

> extras   characters   a classic   a scene   the cast   a best-seller
> the author   a star   a performance   a thriller   the plot   a flop
> a chapter   a role   a script   a masterpiece   a box-office hit
> the stage   an act

Now get into groups and check that your answers are the same.

Useful language

Use the language below to talk to others in your group about a book you have read or a film you have seen recently.

Film
The film is directed/produced by...
It is set in...
It stars...
The role of X is played by...
It portrays/shows...
It conveys a sense of...
X gives a superb/thrilling/
   disappointing performance...
I can thoroughly recommend...
I found the plot rather weak/
   unconvincing

Book
It is extremely readable/rather
   heavy
It is illustrated by...
It is a beautifully written novel
It is published by...
It tells the story of...
The plot centres on...

Writing

1 The summary below comes from a book of short reviews, aimed at those who want help in choosing home videos. Use the prompts to build up a complete text.

EXORCIST The
Based / best-selling novel / William Peter Blatty / 'The Exorcist' / set off / scare / life / audience / and / it / certainly / succeed! Film / have / enormous success / when / first / come out / 1970s / make / it / one / top / money-making films / history / cinema.

A 12-year-old girl / prosperous town / Washington DC / become / possessed / devils. She / finally / save / when / evil spirits / exorcise / and / drive / her body.

Directed / William Friedkin, / it / be / remarkably / well-written film. It / also / uniformly / well-acted / throughout / and / actress / Linda Blair / be / very convincing / deranged child.
Some ways / 'The Exorcist' / be / familiar / blood and thunder / film / but / it / be / much more compelling / many / that genre. If / you / like / horror films, / you / love / 'The Exorcist' – but / not watch / alone!

2 Write a review of a film you have seen recently for the class noticeboard (250 words). You may like to use the ideas given on the next page, or you can use your own ideas if you prefer. Read the Summary box at the end of the unit before you begin.

Introduction

Was the film based on fact? If so, do you know anything about the background to the film? If the film is pure fiction, will you:

- begin with a positive or negative judgement?
- begin with a seemingly contradictory statement?
- use another of the styles illustrated in the 'Opening paragraphs' exercise?

Plot

What happens? Remember to use the present tenses. Try not to ramble or make your account so long that the reader has difficulty in following events.

A general consideration of the film

Who starred in the film? Was the acting convincing? Was it well directed? Comment on as many aspects of the film as you can.

A recommendation

Do you feel the film will appeal to most people? Why/Why not?

3 Some people in your class would like help in choosing a suitable English reader novel to read in their free time. Write a review of a book which you have read recently and enjoyed. (Your review could be included in a class guide to British/American books.)

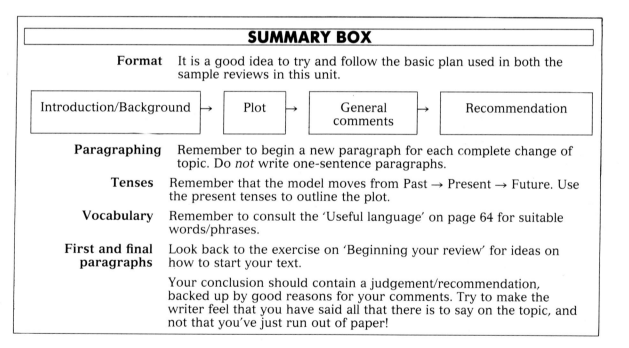

SUMMARY BOX

Format It is a good idea to try and follow the basic plan used in both the sample reviews in this unit.

Introduction/Background → Plot → General comments → Recommendation

Paragraphing Remember to begin a new paragraph for each complete change of topic. Do *not* write one-sentence paragraphs.

Tenses Remember that the model moves from Past → Present → Future. Use the present tenses to outline the plot.

Vocabulary Remember to consult the 'Useful language' on page 64 for suitable words/phrases.

First and final paragraphs Look back to the exercise on 'Beginning your review' for ideas on how to start your text.

Your conclusion should contain a judgement/recommendation, backed up by good reasons for your comments. Try to make the writer feel that you have said all that there is to say on the topic, and not that you've just run out of paper!

Writing a Report

To start you thinking
Work in groups to discuss the following questions.

1 Have you ever had any dealings with the police, either in Britain or in any other country? Why? What happened?

2 Have you ever been the victim of a crime or accident, such as a car crash? Have you ever been a witness? What do the police usually do immediately after a crime has been committed? If you are the victim or a witness, what might they ask you to do?

3 How many different kinds of crime can you think of?

A police statement
With your partner, read through the dialogue below. It is an interview between the victim of a burglary and a policeman sent to deal with the incident.

POLICEMAN:	Right, Mrs Quick, this shouldn't take too long. If you wouldn't mind answering a few questions and I'll jot down a few notes, OK?
MRS QUICK:	Yes, of course – only it all happened so fast, I just don't know if I can really remember that much.
POLICEMAN:	Don't worry. Let's just run through it slowly. Can you remember exactly what time you got home? 5
MRS QUICK:	Well now, let me think . . . it must have been about 7.30 p.m. I got stuck in the traffic – you know, the usual hold-ups on the M25. Anyway, I remember hearing the music for 'Eastenders' coming from Bill's flat – he lives under me, you know. Always has his TV blaring. I think he's a bit deaf, actually. 10
POLICEMAN:	I see. Well now, you went up to your flat – what happened then?
MRS QUICK:	Well, I went to put my keys in the lock – it was a bit tricky 'cause my hands were full of shopping – and I suddenly realised there was something wrong. Someone had obviously had a go at it with a chisel or something.
POLICEMAN:	Uh huh. Go on! 15
MRS QUICK:	Well, anyway, I gave the door a push and it swung open – then I heard a noise and I realised there was someone in my flat!
POLICEMAN:	I see. Did you actually get a look at this person? A man, was it?
MRS QUICK:	Yes, . . . I didn't get a very good look at him really. It was quite dark in the flat, you see. 20
POLICEMAN:	OK. Well, don't worry about it. Just tell me anything you can remember.
MRS QUICK:	All right, er . . . he was about five foot ten or eleven, I should think . . . well-built. Oh yes, and he had quite long hair . . . rather greasy-looking, I remember. I think he was wearing jeans . . . and a dark-coloured jumper.
POLICEMAN:	Yes? Anything else? 25
MRS QUICK:	No, I'm afraid not. Like I said, it was so dark, you see.
POLICEMAN:	OK – something might come back to you later. Now, what was the man doing when you saw him?
MRS QUICK:	Well, he was going through the drawers of my desk. Of course, there was nothing of any value in them, thank goodness. Anyway I shouted something, 30 I forget what . . . and ran downstairs for help. And when we got back up, he'd cleared off – probably got out through the bathroom window – I always leave it open – and then he could have got onto the flat roof of Jim's garage. That's Jim Baker, Flat 26.
POLICEMAN:	Right. Perhaps we could go and have a look in a minute? Now, what's 35 missing?
MRS QUICK:	Well, I don't think he's taken anything actually. I must have caught him when he'd just started . . .

Vocabulary

Phrasal verbs / Verbs + prepositions

1 The verbs on the left below come from the interview on the previous page. Look at how they are used in the text and then match each verb with its correct definition:

a) to clear off
b) to have a go (at)
c) to come back
d) to get stuck
e) to run through
f) to go through
g) to get (something) down

i) to return to memory
ii) to explain/describe something from beginning to end
iii) to be unable to go any further
iv) to check/search carefully
v) to go away
vi) to write something
vii) to attack

2 Now fill in the blanks with an appropriate verb from the list in 1 above.

a) I can't remember his name now but I'm sure it _____ later!
b) John kept pestering her at the disco last night so in the end she told him to _____ .
c) I didn't finish the maths paper because I _____ on the last question.
d) Graham's father has got a black eye because someone at his factory lost his temper and _____ him.
e) When you've finished your composition, _____ it again and check you haven't made any careless mistakes.

Summarising information

1 Read the first two paragraphs of the statement below which the policeman took down during the interview. Notice that it is written in the first person (*I...*).

POLICE STATEMENT
STATEMENT OF: Mrs H Quick
WHERE TAKEN: 16, Court Road, Watford
DATE: 5th October 1990
DATE OF BIRTH: 16.1.1954
OCCUPATION: Accounts clerk
HOME ADDRESS: As above
BUSINESS/HOLIDAY ADDRESS: Quicktel Ltd, 23A Bond Street, Watford
TEL. NOS:
  HOME: 592 6696
  BUSINESS: 578 2493

This statement, consisting of ...... pages each signed by me, is true to the best of my knowledge and belief and I make it knowing that, if it is tendered in evidence, I shall be liable to prosecution if I have wilfully stated in it anything which I know to be false or do not believe to be true.

Dated the 5th day of October, 1990 (signed) Hilary Quick

I arrived home at approximately 7.30 pm Tuesday night, having been delayed by the usual hold-ups on the M25. I know it was about 7.30 pm because I can remember hearing the introductory music for 'Eastenders' coming from the downstairs flat. On reaching the door of my flat, I started to get out my key and then I noticed that the lock on the door had been damaged. Someone had obviously attacked it with a chisel or something. I pushed the door and it opened by itself. Then I heard a noise and I realised there was someone in my flat.

(signed).........................

Taken by .... Time...................... Date..................

---

2 Writing a report involves summarising events and/or conversations. It may also involve changing language into a rather more formal style than the original.

Working with your neighbour, look at the first paragraph of the report and compare it with the actual interview.

a) Which details has the policeman left out of his statement? Why?
b) What sort of words/phrases has he omitted or changed? Why?

3 With your partner, look back to the original interview and note down the important points which you think should be included in the final two paragraphs of the statement. Then write out the rest of the statement in about 120 words.

Reporting language

You are probably already familiar with reported speech forms, for example:

'I didn't do it.'   'I love you, John.'
He said he didn't do it.   *She told John she loved him.*

However we can sometimes make our account more vivid by using special reporting verbs. The following verbs are often used to report or to summarise speech:

to wonder if ...	to request that ...
to urge (someone) to ...	to congratulate (someone) (on) ...
to mention that ...	to propose that ...
to announce (that) ...	to point out (that) ...
to remind ...	to claim (that) ...
to agree (that) ...	to deny (that) ...
to protest (that) ...	to explain (that) ...
to refuse (to) ...	to object (that) ...
to state (that) ...	to express one's admiration/
to express concern that ...	surprise/relief (at) (that) ...

1 Can you add any more to the list?

2 Fill in the blanks with a suitable reporting verb (there is sometimes more than one possible answer).

a) 'Go on! Buy it!'
   He_____ her to buy it.

b) 'But I don't sing off-key! That's just not true!'
   She _____ she didn't sing off-key.

c) 'It's like this, you see – if I give *you* a pay-rise everyone will want one. It's out of the question, I'm afraid!
   His employer _____ to give him a pay-rise.

d) 'Good news, everyone! We're getting married.'
   Paul and Sally _____ their marriage.

e) 'No, I'm afraid I'm not prepared to do any overtime. It's not in my contract.'
   She _____ to doing any overtime.

f) 'Well done, Tom.'
   She _____ Tom.

g) 'But according to you, the hotel was supposed to be 5-star!'
   You _____ the hotel was 5-star.

h) 'I didn't say any such thing!'
   He _____ saying it.

i) 'Yes, I know you're disappointed. But if you'd done more work, you know, you could have passed.'
His instructor _____ he could have passed with more hard work.

j) 'Really? Good old Roger! I never thought he'd do it.'
He _____ at Roger's success.

Reporting meetings/ discussions

When writing reports, it is important not to include irrelevant details or comments. Here are the minutes (i.e. a written report) of a meeting of the local youth club. The usual minute-taker is ill and another person has taken on the job. However they have included some inappropriate details. With your partner, look at the first part of the minutes and cross out anything which you feel is irrelevant or inappropriate.

Youth club meeting

CHRIS: Right, let's get started then. First of all, thanks for coming on such a foul evening – I'm sure it was quite a struggle so thanks for making the effort! Now, we've got to be out of the hall by 10 o'clock prompt tonight – the vicar's got one of his important meetings tomorrow morning and he wants everything spick and span by then. Don't hang around or you'll get roped in to help with cleaning! Anyway, keep your contributions brief, if you can please.

Er... we've got just one apology for absence, I see. Clare Jones. (Actually I know John has taken her off to the theatre as a surprise 21st present, so let's hope she's enjoying it!)

Anyone seen the minutes of the last meeting? Yes? Are they going round? Great! Any comments on them?

JIM: Yes, I've got a query. Why has the coach trip to London been cancelled?

CHRIS: Well, actually, nobody seems that interested – we've sold very few tickets, not enough to make it worthwhile, really.

RON: Well, I think it's a real shame! I was really looking forward to going round Soho and having a real binge[1].

JANE: Yes, it would be nice to go sometime. Perhaps we could go in the summer? The weather will be better then, with a bit of luck!

---

[1]*binge*: good time

> ### MINUTES OF YOUTH CLUB MEETING HELD ON 5TH JANUARY 1991
>
> *The chairman (Chris) opened the meeting and thanked everyone for coming on such a cold evening. He was sure it was quite a struggle. He urged everyone to keep their contributions brief as the church hall had to be vacated by 10 p.m. prompt because the vicar needed to get in to clean it for another meeting the next morning.*
>
> ***Apologies for absence*** *from Clare Jones. She had gone to the theatre for a birthday celebration with her boyfriend, John. It was a surprise for her 21st so Chris said he hoped she was enjoying it.*
>
> ***Minutes of the last meeting*** *These were circulated.*
>
> ***Matters arising*** *Jim asked why the coach trip to London had been cancelled and Chris explained that there was a lack of interest and insufficient tickets had been sold. Ron said he thought it was a shame. He'd been looking forward to going round Soho and having a real binge. It was suggested that another trip be organised for the summer when the weather would be better (with a bit of luck!).*

Writing

1 Study the pictures below carefully. They show events during a recent hijack. Work with your partner. Decide first who is A and who is B.

A: you are one of the hostages released from the plane

B: you are from the security police – you are going to question A closely about events leading up to and during the hijack

Together, write up a report on what happened for police files.

2 In the following dialogue a teacher is speaking to her primary school class. Put the dialogue into reported speech. Begin like this:

Miss Jones checked whether everyone remembered what...

'Now everyone, do you remember what you have to bring for the school trip tomorrow?'

'Yes, miss!'

'Even you, Sammy? I'm amazed! Perhaps you could tell me again what you'll be bringing.'

'Sandwiches, Miss. And my swimming costume.'

'Well done Sammy! Anything else?'

'Mm...My project sheet, Miss...and a pencil and a rubber.'

'Ah, you do intend doing some work after all then, Sammy – thank goodness for that! All night then everybody, you can go now – but remember to go to bed early tonight and to be on time tomorrow. The coach leaves at 9 a.m. sharp – anyone who's not there on time, doesn't go! So be warned!'

3 Look at the text below. On the left you will see the actual words used in a sports club meeting. The text on the right is the first part of the minutes.

a) With your partner, decide which of the reporting verbs you practised in the previous exercise could be used in the minutes.
b) Complete the minutes (notice that the style is quite formal).

Sports club meeting

JOE: Well, good evening everyone and thanks for coming. We've got quite a lengthy agenda for this evening so I'd be grateful if you could keep your comments brief and to the point! Now, first of all, last Sunday's sponsored bike-ride for Children in Need. I know you'll all be delighted to hear that we raised £800! So, well done, all you cyclists.

SALLY: Wow! That's fantastic!

TOM: Yes, that's marvellous!

MINUTES OF MEETING 10TH MAY 1991
The chairman opened the meeting by welcoming those present and urging members to keep their comments brief as there was a lengthy agenda.

Sponsored bike-ride (Sunday 5th May)
The chairman announced that £800 had been raised and congratulated all those who took part. This was seconded by other members present although Chris...

CHRIS: Hear! hear! A great effort! Er..., I've got one slight criticism, though. As I see it, we wasted a brilliant chance for raising extra money on Sunday. I mean the riders had nothing to identify them – like arm-bands or T-shirts or anything – so none of the people around knew what the ride was for. I mean, they might have given us some money on the spot if they'd known.

SALLY: Yes, you've got a point there. The trouble is, we never seem to leave ourselves enough time to do things properly! I mean...

DICK: Now, hang on a minute! Be fair! I mean, I know everything was a bit rushed this time but that was because our last two meetings were cancelled. Surely you don't blame me for that!

JOE: Now, come along please everyone calm down. Perhaps we could move on to the next item. As you know, we've had to postpone...

SUMMARY BOX

Being concise	Do not include irrelevant details in your report. Always check your first draft and be ready to cross out non-essential information. Remember how to summarise information.
Register	Reports and minutes tend to be very formal. Check that your language is not too colloquial or 'chatty'.
Reporting speech	Remember to use a variety of reporting verbs. Check with the list on page 68 if you are not sure which to use.

Writing a Narrative

To start you
thinking

Get into groups to discuss the following questions.

1 Suspense stories and thrillers are very popular, even though they can be disturbing or frightening. Why do you think this is? Do you like thrillers? Can you think of a good example of a thriller you have seen or read? What was it about? What is it in a good thriller that makes you want to watch/read on?

2 Some people have phobias about certain things. Do you? Do you have phobias about any kinds of animals/insects? Why do you think people have such irrational fears?

A short story

The extract below comes from a short story, 'The Rain Horse' by Ted Hughes, a modern British poet and writer. It is the nightmare story of a horse which becomes attacker, as if possessed by an evil spirit.

A young man revisits the countryside he has not seen for twelve years. Alone in the fields and in the driving rain, he realises that he is being watched...

1   At the wood top, with the silvered grey light coming in behind it, the black horse was standing under the trees, its head high and alert, its ears pricked, watching him.

2   A horse sheltering from the rain generally goes into a sort of stupor[1], hangs its head and lets its eyelids droop, and so it stays as long as the rain lasts. This horse was nothing like that. It was watching him intently, standing perfectly still, its neck and flank[2] shining in the hard light.

3   He turned back. His scalp[3] went icy and he shivered. What was he to do? Ridiculous to try driving it away. And to leave the wood, with the rain still coming down, was out of the question. Meanwhile the idea of being watched became more and more unsettling[4] until at last he had to twist around again, to see if the horse had moved. It stood exactly as before.

4   This was absurd. He took control of himself and turned back, determined not to give the horse one more thought. If it wanted to share the wood with him, let it. If it wanted to stare at him, let it. He was nestling firmly into these resolutions when the ground shook and he heard the crash of a heavy body coming down the wood. Like lightning his legs bounded him upright. The horse was almost on top of him, its head stretching forwards, ears flattened and lips lifted back from the long yellow teeth. He got one snapshot glimpse of the red-veined eyeball as he flung himself backwards around the tree. Then he was away up the slope, twisting between the close trees till he tripped and sprawled. He spun around, sat up and looked back, ready to scramble off in a flash to one side. He was panting from the sudden excitement and effort. The horse had disappeared. The wood was empty except for the drumming, slant grey rain.

5   He got up, furious. Knocking the dirt and leaves from his suit as well as he could he looked around for a weapon. The horse was evidently mad, had an abscess[5] on its brain or something of the sort. Or maybe it was just spiteful[6]. Rain sometimes puts creatures into queer[7] states. Whatever it was, he was going to get away from the wood as quickly as possible, rain or no rain...

[1]*stupor*: state in which one cannot use the senses
[2]*flank*: side of horse
[3]*scalp*: skin on the top of the head
[4]*unsettling*: worrying
[5]*abscess*: swelling in or on the body
[6]*spiteful*: desiring to annoy
[7]*queer*: strange, abnormal

Comprehension check

1 Where, exactly, was the horse when the young man realised it was watching him?

2 How was its behaviour different from normal?

3 Why did the attack take the young man by surprise?

4 How did he try to explain the attack to himself after the horse had disappeared?

Analysis

Work in pairs to answer the following questions.

1 What is the function of the first two paragraphs of the extract? Which verb tenses are used here? Why?

2 In the first two paragraphs, the writer convinces us of the reality of the horse. How does he do this?

3 Which tenses are used to describe the actual attack by the horse (line 18)? Pick out the verbs used to describe the young man's rush to escape. Check that you understand them.

4 In the story, the horse returns. What do you imagine happens next? How would you finish the story? Discuss your ideas with your partner.

Paragraphing

1 Which phrase best summarises each paragraph in the extract?

a) the attack ☐

b) his indecision ☐

c) his attempts to explain the situation ☐

d) setting the scene/the background ☐

e) the unusual behaviour of the horse ☐

2 Narratives usually follow a similar time sequence.

Is this true of the extract you have just read?

Being dramatic!

1 We sometimes start a sentence with phrases like this when we want to give a sense of drama.

> ***Like lightning,* his legs bounded him upright.**

Work with your partner to match the following:

a) Not daring to move,
b) With hardly a sound,
c) Never stopping to look back,
d) In the nick of time,
e) Like a bolt from the blue,

i) the thought hit him that Val must have fired the shot.
ii) she stared in horror at the snake, now only feet away.
iii) the fire brigade arrived and got the fire under control.
iv) he crept into the silent room.
v) she ran desperately through the tangled undergrowth.

2 Complete the following in a suitable way.

a) Quick as a flash, he _____

b) Without stopping to think, she _____

c) Hardly daring to breathe, he _____

d) In barely a whisper, she _____

e) Without a word of warning, he _____

Can you think of any similar phrases?

3 We can use inversion to make sentences more dramatic. Change the sentences below, in the same way.

> ***Hardly** had he got his breath back, when the horse appeared again.*

a) She'd never heard a dog howl like that before.
   Never before _____

b) The sound of tapping had barely stopped when a new sound began.
   Barely _____

c) I heard the footsteps again. I'd scarcely reached the corner.
   Scarcely _____

d) He reached the top of the hill. The storm broke.
   Hardly _____

e) He shouldn't be told under any circumstances.
   Under no circumstances _____

Connecting sentences

The sentences below come from a very different style of text. Work with your partner to put them into the correct order. The underlined words should help you to do this. Where do you think the story comes from: a novel, a police report, a newspaper, a letter? Give reasons for your answer. You may like to copy and cut up the text for this exercise.

a)	*'All the same,* I keep wondering what would have happened if it had been a child or a pensioner instead of me.'	☐
b)	*She* ran round to the other side of her car but, *to her horror,* she saw that *they* were following her.	☐
c)	The owner voiced *the same fears* although she claimed that the dogs had never attacked anyone prior to this incident.	☐
d)	*He* popped into some public toilets as the couple were about to drive home.	☐
e)	*'She* brought *them* to heel very quickly and was very apologetic', said Mrs Kirtland.	☐
f)	*A terrified housewife* fought off an attack by two Alsatians with her handbag yesterday.	☐
g)	The nightmare *finally* ended when the dogs' owner – believed to be a holiday-maker – called the Alsatians off.	☐
h)	She *then* hit out at them with her handbag but they went for that as well.	☐
i)	*Nevertheless,* she plans to have both of them put down in the near future, rather than risk a second and possibly more tragic occurrence.	☐
j)	*Then,* out of nowhere, two ferocious dogs appeared and went straight for her.	☐
k)	*Meanwhile,* Mrs Kirtland walked on towards the car.	☐
l)	*The dogs* suddenly went for Mrs Jan Kirtland (47) at Milford while she was out for a walk with her husband, Bruce.	☐

Text comparison

Before you start writing any type of narrative, it is important to remember the sort of audience you are writing for. An imaginative short story demands a very different kind of style to a factual report. With your partner, decide which text – 'The Rain Horse' or the text on page 74 – contains the following:

1 a highly personalised account of what happened
2 very descriptive adjectives and verbs
3 exact details of names and places
4 simple, straightforward language, which is easy to read
5 a heightened sense of suspense
6 short, clear paragraphs
7 short, agitated sentences
8 a neutral tone
9 sudden, unanswered questions

Beginnings and endings

1 Do you remember the normal time sequence for a narrative? Look back to page 73 if you are not sure.

2 One of the most difficult things to do when writing a narrative is to find a good way to begin, so that you arouse the curiosity and interest of the reader.

The picture below shows a yacht which was wrecked during a heavy storm. Imagine that you and your family/friends were out sailing on the yacht when the storm broke. You have been asked to write about your experiences for the newsletter of your local club. How would you begin your story? Work in groups to write a good introduction. Look at the 'ideas' below before you begin.

Ideas
Avoid childish beginnings, for example:

It was a nice day when we set out and the sun was shining...

Try to imagine you were really there at the start of the trip. Ask yourself questions like:

When? Where? How many of you were there?
What were your feelings/plans/expectations for the day?
What previous experience did you all have?
What preparations had you made?
Describe the sea/the weather/the yacht.

When you have finished, decide which group has written the most effective paragraph(s). Say why you have made your choice.

3 Now discuss how you would continue your story.

4 It is very important to supply a good, well-rounded ending to your narrative so that the reader comes away satisfied that the outcome/future implications of events have been fully explored. A disappointing ending can ruin a good story! In your groups, write an ending to the yachting disaster story, starting from the point where rescue was at hand.

Text correction With your partner, see how many mistakes you can find in the composition below. Can you suggest a better way to paragraph the text?

<u>My earliest memories</u>

My memories start from when I was 4 years old. It is a terrible memory, I can't forget it. One night, when I was 4 years old, my house caught fire one night. And everything burned out. When my parents noticed that our house was burning, I and my elder brother were sleeping in our beds. As our room was on upstair, so we didn't know what was going on with my house at all. But my parents were very upset, and they ran out of the house without us. Then my mother remembered about me and my brother. She ran into the burning house and went up the stairs to help us, and hold me and brother in her arms, and ran out of the house again.

When we succeded to ran out of the house I woke up. I saw a terrible scene. The house was burning and I felt very scared.

And the smoke made my brother's throat so bad that he couldn't speak well for a month after the fire. Even now, I can still remember that terrible scene clearly.

Writing

1 Write the story of the yachting disaster in full, using the ideas you have already worked with.

2 Write a letter to a friend in about 300 words describing an event, pleasant or unpleasant, in which you were involved. Write only the body of the letter, not the address, etc. You may like to include the following ideas:

Introduction Where and when did this happen? Who was involved?
Development Describe the events in sequence (be as dramatic as you can!)
Conclusion What was the outcome of the event? Why has it made such a great impression on you?

Before you begin to write, look at the Summary box at the end of this unit.

3 Write an article for a class magazine (about 300 words) entitled 'A day to remember', describing an exciting/thrilling event in your life. The story can be true or imaginary.

SUMMARY BOX

Format Try to follow the plan you have seen in this unit:

| Background | → | Events | → | Result/Sequel |

Being dramatic Writing a story from imagination usually requires a sense of the dramatic. Look back to the exercise on pages 73/4 for ideas on how to make your sentences more vivid. Short, agitated sentences can heighten the sense of drama. Remember also how important good beginnings and endings are.

Tenses The past perfect (*had done/had been doing*) and the past continuous (*was doing*) are often used in the opening paragraph(s) of a story for setting the scene. Remember to use the simple past tense for relating dramatic events.

Guidelines and Instructions

To start you thinking

1 Environmental issues are very much in the news these days. How worried are you about the environment? Can you name some of the problems which worry people?

2 What do you do in your own life to help protect the environment (if anything)? Do you take empty bottles to a bottle bank, buy 'green' products in the shops, etc.?

Simple guidelines

Read the guidelines on 'Going Green' below. How many of the things listed do you already do? Can you add any more ideas to the list?

🐋 GO GREEN! 🐋

So we've convinced you! You want to go green. Here are 10 simple things to help you get started.

1 Have your car converted to unleaded petrol.

2 Leave wild flowers alone – don't dig them up.

3 Take your bottles to the bottle bank.

4 Start using recycled products whenever possible.

5 Start checking those aerosols, make sure they are ozone friendly.

6 Start using beauty products that haven't caused cruelty to animals.

7 Visit your health food shop more often – they can be Aladdin's caves of chemical-free and environment-friendly goods.

8 Start buying organic foods or grow your own if you can.

9 Start scrutinising labels more thoroughly.

10 Start protesting. If a particular subject gets you hot under the collar write to your MP or councillor, whichever is appropriate. The only way to get something done is to make yourself heard!

Layout

1 Why do you think the writer of this article has written his tips out as a numbered list rather than a connected paragraph?

2 Where do you think the article comes from? Who is it aimed at?

Detailed guidelines Now look at the guidelines below on how to beat exam stress. With your partner, decide on the appropriate heading for each section.

A STUDENTS' GUIDE TO EXAM STRESS

As exam fever hots up, keep your cool with tips from our health correspondent Dr Barry Lynch.

a Stress is difficult to define but most of us know it when we experience it. We may have mental symptoms: panic, feeling trapped or overwhelmed. Or there may be physical symptoms: sweating palms, butterflies, headaches, breathlessness or sleeplessness.

b Stress can cause us to feel overwhelmed and powerless to tackle the very things that are causing the stress in the first place. So make a carefully written plan and the problems will seem less overwhelming. Ticking off each thing as you do it will help you feel there is light at the end of the tunnel.

c When you're writing your revision plan, make sure you include some time off - exactly an hour or whatever - before you go back to work. Look forward to your time off and do something pleasant in it. Work out little treats and rewards for yourself as you tick off each thing on your plan. The treats can be simple: an ice cream, half an hour listening to your personal stereo, or walking the dog.

d Easier said than done, I know, but exercise is one of the best ways of relaxing: it's the natural way to deal with adrenaline and similar hormones that are rushing around your body. A walk will help; a quick swim or half an hour of tennis or another game is even better.

e *Don't* drink endless cups of tea or coffee: although caffeine is a stimulant it will eventually only make you more tense and nervy.
Don't try to go without sleep - sleep is a natural way of relieving stress.
Don't be tempted to use alcohol or other drugs to relieve stress. They create more problems than they solve.

- TIME OFF
- ACTION KILLS WORRY
- RECOGNISE THE SYMPTOMS
- THINGS TO AVOID
- LEARN HOW TO RELAX

Format 1 In this article the writer has used a rather different format from the one in the 'Go Green' article. How do the two articles differ in terms of a) content and b) layout?

2 Who is the writer of the second article? How does the style of his article reflect his purpose in writing?

Useful language In the next exercise you are going to write your own tips/guidelines. First write down any language from the two models which you think may be useful for a similar text (e.g. *Don't...,... will help you to...*). What do you notice about the form of the verbs used most for giving instructions?

Writing your own guidelines You have been asked to write a set of guidelines similar to the 'Students' Guide to Exam Stress' article for your local English-speakers' magazine on one of the topics below. Get into groups and prepare instructions for one of the headings (each group should choose a different heading).

Topics

1 Preparing for your foreign holiday
2 A guide to healthy living
3 Looking after the countryside
4 Dealing with a difficult teenager
5 A guide to safety in the home

When you have finished, get into new groups and exchange guideline sheets. Comment on the content and style of each.

Instructions

The text on the opposite page contains some 'Do It Yourself' advice on building a garden pond for people who wish to attract wildlife to their gardens. Read the text and underline the language used to give advice/instructions, e.g. *You can ...*, *Remember that ... .*

Comprehension

1 Why should you think carefully before deciding on the site of your pond?

2 Why do you need to leave space at the shallow end of the pond?

3 Where shouldn't you take your plants from? Why not?

Style

Notice that the writer of this text uses a relaxed 'chatty' style. He is writing for people who may not be technically minded and who need to be encouraged to feel the job (i.e. making a pond) is easy enough for them to try, for example:

Informal 'chatty' style	Formal/technical style
You will need to put in a lining	*Put in a lining*
You will have to find a good place for the pond	*Find a good place for the pond*
Plants are best collected from friends	*Collect plants from friends*

Can you suggest any other ways in which this text appears more informal than a typical set of technical instructions?

Useful language

Tick off the language of advice/instruction which you have already underlined in the text.

☐ If you ... you will
☐ You can ...
☐ Remember that ...
☐ You will have to ...
☐ Keep in mind that/what ...
☐ You ought to (not to) ...
☐ You will need to ...
☐ Don't ...
☐ You should ...

☐ Don't forget to ...
☐ Make sure you ...
☐ Be careful to (not to) ...
☐ Try to avoid ... otherwise ...
☐ It's a good idea to ...
☐ This is especially important if/when ...
☐ Whatever you do, don't ...

Can you add any more to the list?

Giving informal instructions

Imagine that a friend has asked you for some instructions on one of the following:

1 Making a campfire
2 Playing a party game (you choose the game)
3 Making a simple recipe

Practise telling your neighbour how to carry out the task you have chosen. (You will be writing the instructions later in this unit.)

MAKING A POND

Birds need water to drink and to bath in - but a pond will attract much more than just birds and will provide a home for many other creatures too. If you make your own pond, you will have extra enjoyment because you can watch it improve as plants grow and new creatures find it and move in. You can keep a record of everything as it happens.

THINK FIRST!

First, you will have to find the best place for your pond. Keep in mind what might happen if it floods in winter; remember that it could be dangerous for very small children; remember that you ought not to attract birds if
10 you have bird-hunting cats. You will also need space for the soil you dig out, which might be difficult to move later.

WHAT TO DO

Mark the edges of your pond on the ground with pegs and
15 string. Then dig it out, putting the soil well away to one side if you can. Make the hole deep at one end and shallow at the other. Remember that you will have to put in a lining, a covering of soil, and some plants, so leave plenty of depth even in parts which you want to be
20 shallow in the end.

PLANT IT UP

Plants are best collected from friends and neighbours who already have ponds, or from garden centres. Don't dig up wild ones. You can also find someone with a pond
25 which attracts frogs and ask for some frogspawn to start off a colony of your own - don't collect it from natural sites. Friends may also provide you with some pond snails.

WAIT AND SEE!

30 Then sit back and see what happens! Keep a record of birds and other animals at your pond - and note any flowers which might grow naturally. You should have plenty to see for years to come.

Connectors

1 Time connectors (*First . . .*, *Next . . .*, etc.) can be very useful for linking lists of instructions. In the following recipe the sentences have been 'jumbled', but the time connectors will help you to put them in the right order. Work with your neighbour to reassemble the text correctly.

	Roast leg of lamb	
a)	*When cooked* remove the lamb from the oven, keep it hot and let it rest for 20 minutes.	☐
b)	*Meanwhile* make the gravy.	☐
c)	*Next* put the sliced onion and thyme in a roasting tin and put the leg of lamb on top.	☐
d)	*First* heat the oven to 190° C, 375° F, Gas Mark 5.	☐
e)	*When* the 5 minutes is up, strain the gravy through a sieve until it is clear and serve boiling hot.	☐
f)	*To start with* skim most of the used fat from the roasting tin, then pour in wine and stock or water and boil for 5 minutes.	☐
g)	*Then* spread butter over the lamb and pour oil over this.	☐
h)	Put the prepared joint into the middle of the oven and roast for 1½ to 2 hours.	☐
i)	*And a final point*; be careful not to allow the lamb or the gravy to go cold before serving, as the fat becomes granular and hard as it cools.	☐

2 Make a list of the time connectors used in the text above. Can you think of any others?

Being concise

Compare the instructions in the recipe above with those used in the 'Making a pond' text on page 81. In what way are the instructions different? Which text is the more concise and technical? Why?

Tenses

Passive forms

When giving instructions we are usually more interested in the action than in the person carrying it out. Written instructions therefore often involve the use of the passive, for example:

> You should line the pond.
> *The pond should be lined.*

Put the following into the passive:

1 You shouldn't build the house on that site.
2 Make sure you switch the electricity off before you begin.
3 You ought not to paint the surface until you have removed the old wood.
4 You will need to have prepared the sauce the night before.
5 You will have to plan the work carefully some weeks in advance.

Writing

1 You have been asked to write some guidelines (similar to those you practised on page 79) in English for new students who are coming to your school/college. Write an advice sheet which can be handed to them on their first day. You can include guidance on areas suggested below, but include your own ideas too.

punctuality	absence from school
homework	extra-curricular activities
smoking	what to do if you have a problem
the library	things to avoid
precautions you should take	

2 *Either*

a) Jot down some informal instructions for one of the tasks which you practised on page 80.

or

b) Write concise instructions on 'How to mend a puncture' to accompany the pictures below.

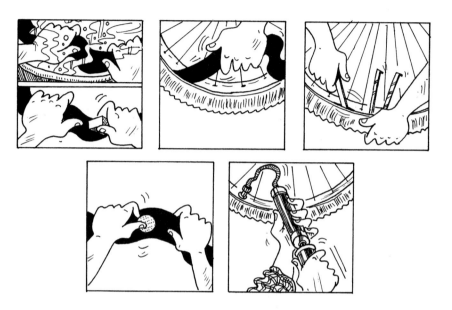

Look at the Summary box at the end of this unit before you begin to write.

3 Some British friends are staying in the house next door to you for a short holiday and want to make a barbecue in the garden. They have never had a barbecue before. Write down some instructions/tips for them on how to make up the fire and how to prepare and cook the food.

SUMMARY BOX

Layout	Always consider your reasons for writing and the person you are writing for when choosing the layout of your text. If you are giving simple, undetailed tips, a numbered list may be a good idea. If you are giving longer guidelines/instructions, you may need to divide your text into clearly headed sections.
Style	Decide whether you are writing in an informal 'chatty' style or a more formal 'technical' style and use appropriate language.
Instruction language	Remember that the imperative form is most commonly used, particularly in concise, technical instructions. If you are giving tips to friends or do not want to sound too technical, remember to use some of the phrases from the 'Useful language' section on page 80. Don't forget that the passive is also a useful verb form for giving instructions.
Connectors	Use connectors (*First...*, *Next...*, etc.) when possible, especially when writing a set of concise instructions. Look back to the list you made on page 82 if necessary.

Writing a Newspaper Report

To start you thinking

Discuss the following questions in pairs.

1 Have you read a British newspaper   a) today,   b) this month,   c) this year or   d) never?

2 In Britain, many people buy a daily paper. How often do you read a national paper in your country? Do you prefer a really serious 'quality' paper or a 'popular' one?

3 How many British newspapers can you name? Which ones are 'quality' papers and which ones belong to the 'popular' press? What are the basic differences between them?

A newspaper report

Now read the article below and decide whether you think it comes from a popular or a quality newspaper.

999 SHAMBLES AS POLICE MOVE IN

Police and first-aiders battled to provide a makeshift ambulance service for Londoners yesterday.

All but nine of the capital's 71 ambulance stations were closed as the pay dispute escalated.

London's chief ambulance officer admitted the service was 'a shambles'.

Police vehicles and St John Ambulance vans equipped with stretchers and first aid kits struggled to keep up with 999 calls.

Late last night police had dealt with 400 emergencies.

An eleven-year-old Brixton girl whose hand was severed in an accident was taken to hospital by a neighbour while a fire engine followed with her fingers packed in ice.

Last night Union Leader Roger Poole attacked hospital managers for 'showing contempt for their employees'.

London's fire brigade said injured people could be taken to hospital by fire engines if the waiting time for an ambulance was considered too long.

Talks aimed at breaking the London deadlock broke down after just 30 minutes last night.

Vocabulary

Look at how the words below are used in the text. Write down what you think they mean, then check your answers in a dictionary.

1 battled (line 1)   5 stretcher (line 13)

2 makeshift (line 2)   6 keep up with (line 15)

3 escalated (line 7)   7 contempt (line 28)

4 shambles (line 10)   8 deadlock (line 37)

Paragraphing

Why do you think the writer has dealt with each point in a separate one-sentence paragraph? What might this style tell you about a typical reader of this paper?

Text comparison

Compare the style of this article with the one below from the *Guardian* of the same day.

Ambulance shambles

**Simon Beavis,
Patrick Wintour
and Gareth Parry**

Attempts to resolve the ambulance dispute in London failed last night as employers admitted that the suspension of staff[1] who had imposed a work-to-rule[2] had reduced services to a shambles, with all but nine of the capital's 71 ambulance stations closed.

Union leaders met managers of the London Ambulance Service to try to hammer out[3] a deal. But the talks broke down, with managers insisting that unions withdraw work-to-rule instructions, including a ban on the use of radio telephones. Shop stewards meet this morning to decide their next move.

Yesterday's events brought the six-week-old national dispute to its most fraught[4] state since unions launched an overtime ban after refusing a 6.5 per cent pay offer. There were indications that staff outside London were considering stepping up their action in a number of areas including Manchester and Berkshire.

Unions have called repeatedly for the dispute to be referred to binding arbitration[5], but Health Service managers have refused.

As ambulance stations were shut, accident and emergency calls were transferred from stations to the ambulance service's central control room in Waterloo and on to the Metropolitan Police, the Red Cross and St John Ambulance services. Police set up a special operations room at New Scotland Yard to deal with emergencies. Thirty Metropolitan police vans were converted into ambulances.

A Scotland Yard spokesman said the more than 60 casualties dealt with ranged from heart attack victims to women in labour.

A fire crew reported that a police ambulance arrived an hour after they had been called to break down the door of a Brixton flat to retrieve an 11-year-old girl's fingers that had been severed by a razor sharp letter box.

Mr Tom Crosby, Chief officer of the London Ambulance Service, conceded at one of a series of press conferences yesterday that the service had been reduced to a shambles. 'It would be a fair description, something we are not very proud of at all on this side of the table', he said.

[1] *suspension of staff*: withholding employment from staff for a time
[2] *work-to-rule*: form of working which causes activity to become slower because attention is paid to every point in the rules
[3] *to hammer out*: to discuss and make a decision about
[4] *fraught*: troubled
[5] *binding arbitration*: judgement by a person or group chosen by both sides, which is compulsory
[6] *shambles*: a state of disorder

Which of the following styles would you find in a) a quality paper and b) a popular paper?

Quality papers   **Popular papers**

a) short, zappy style
b) complex sentence structure
c) high level of vocabulary
d) one-sentence paragraphs
e) down-to-earth language
f) well-developed paragraphs
g) concise details
h) detailed facts

Comprehension

1 What caused the ambulance dispute in London?
2 Why did peace talks break down?
3 Who is answering emergency calls?
4 Why were police called to the Brixton flat?

Paragraphing

1 What is the topic of each of the paragraphs in the *Guardian* article?

2 As we have seen, the writer of this article uses well-developed paragraphs, unlike the one-sentence paragraphs of the *Mirror*. Why do they do this? What do you think the readers of the *Guardian* expect from the articles they read?

Paragraph jumble

1 The article opposite concerns a popular BBC TV series 'Bergerac', in which Jersey detective Jim Bergerac solves a range of crimes including robbery and murder. The paragraphs have been jumbled. Work with a partner to sort out a logical order for the story.

2 The words in italics help to link the text together by referring back to words used earlier in the story. Find the original words, for example:

us: Keith Boleat and his family

Format

The Bergerac article you have just read follows the same basic plan used in many popular and quality newspaper reports. Put the four basic parts of the plan listed below into the correct boxes, following the order used in the articles in this unit.

a) Comments from spokesman
b) Expansion
c) Reference to future developments
d) Summary of story

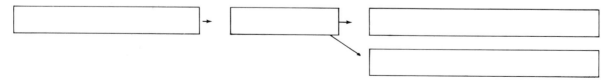

Check your answer with the Summary box at the end of the unit.

BERGERAC TV HORROR PHOTOS SHOCK FAMILY

Murder pictures mystery

BODY BLOW: *One of the 'murder'
photographs*

EXCLUSIVE
BY MURRAY DAVIES

1 *The picture* — showing a body with a vicious head wound and half buried in sand — was among a pile of murder photos on a school playing field.

2 Police immediately launched an investigation into how *the photographs*, apparently taken by police of murder victims, had gone astray.

3 *They* were discovered by plumber Keith Boleat who was out walking with his wife and two-year-old daughter, Melanie, on the holiday island of Jersey.

4 A GRUESOME photo of a murdered man which was found by a shocked family sparked a police probe.

5 A BBC spokesman said: "We are sorry if *the pictures* caused alarm.

6 *The snaps* were to be used during an episode of the hit BBC series.

7 Then a bright copper solved *the mystery*.

8 *They* belonged to Jersey's most famous detective —TV's Jim Bergerac, played by John Nettles.

Fright

9 Mr Boleat said:"The pictures looked all too realistic. It gave *us* the fright of our lives."

STAR: *John Nettles*

Tenses

1 Newspaper articles often contain a wide range of tenses. How many different tenses can you find in the *Guardian* article? With your partner, work out why those tenses are used.

2

> **All but nine of the capital's 71 ambulance stations were closed.**

Why is the passive used in the sentence above? Can you find any more examples in the articles in this unit? Why do you think the passive is found so often in newspaper articles?

3 Read the article below and work with your partner to put the verbs in brackets into the correct form.

Fairy-tale story of whale that thinks a ship is his mother

It [1](be) just like a classic Disney tale. Some time ago a baby whale [2](call) Little Squirt [3](find) himself lost after [4](stray) from his mother's side. For weeks he [5](swim) through the ocean alone unable to trace the school he [6](never leave) before. Then, when all hope [7](seem) lost, he [8](catch) sight of a large black and white object. But there [9](be) a twist in the tail. For it [10](turn out) that Little Squirt [11](befriend) a ferry, [12](believe) it [13](be) his mother.

Now Squirt [14](never leave) the ship's side and [15](snuggle) up to the hull, playfully [16](spray) passengers with water. Passengers and crew [17](be) delighted with him and he [18](now become) so popular that school classes [19](buy) ferry tickets just to get a glimpse.

Killer whale expert Eric Hoyt said: 'When whales [20](get) separated from a school even just by accident they [21](seek out) companionship. I [22](come across) a number of cases of really young whales which [23](befriend) boats, although it [24](be) not everyday behaviour.'

No one [25](know) how long Squirt's touching relationship with the ferry [26](continue). But in the meantime, everyone concerned [27](have) a whale of a time.

Reported speech

The verbs in the box below are often used in newspapers to report speech.

claim	explain	complain	insist	accuse	admit
promise	add	deny	confess	state	beg

Check in your dictionary that you know the meaning of the words, then put the sentences below into reported speech. Do not use the same verb twice.

1 'I tell you, I didn't do it!'
The woman _____

2 'I have just come back from the cinema.'
She _____

3 'All right, all right, so I *did* do it.'
_____

4 'I'll never do it again!'
_____

5 'I murdered him because I hate him.'
_____

6 'He used to come home drunk and beat me up.'
_____

7 'Please, please, can I make one last phone call?'
_____

8 'Look, nobody is listening to what I'm saying!'
_____

Group activity

Get into groups of six to eight for the next exercise. Look at the pictures below and work out a story for each sequence, as if you were preparing for a radio news broadcast. One person in the group will be the newsreader and the others will be reporters/interviewees for each of the stories. When you have rehearsed, you may like to perform your 'news broadcast' in front of the class.

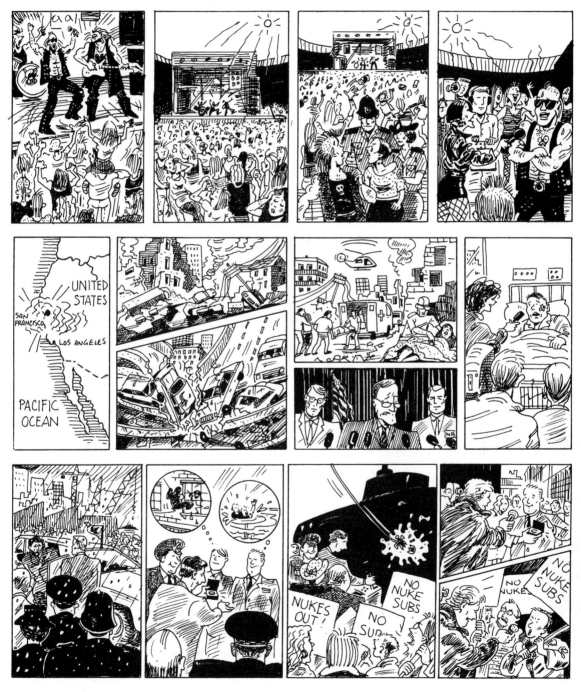

Writing

1 a) Write out the stories you prepared for your news broadcast as they might appear in *either* a) a popular *or* b) a serious newspaper.

b) Imagine you work for a popular newspaper like the *Daily Mirror*. Work with a partner to expand one of the following stories which have just arrived in the news office. Use your imagination to fill out the details. Each article should be approximately 200 words.

i)
> GOVERNMENT RESIGNS STOP NEW ELECTION CALLED FOR JUNE 10TH STOP P.M. BLAMES STRIKES STOP TRANSPORT WORKERS STILL OUT STOP ELECTRICIANS THREATEN TO STOP WORK MIDNIGHT STOP ECONOMY ON KNIFE-EDGE STOP PANIC IN STOCK EXCHANGE STOP CHANCELLOR PLEADS FOR CALM STOP

ii)
> BOY SAVES FRIEND FROM RIVER TRAGEDY STOP BOAT HITS BRIDGE AND SINKS STOP 10 YEAR OLD BOY TRAPPED IN CABIN STOP FRIEND DIVES UNDER AGAIN TO FREE HIM STOP POSSIBLE POLICE COMMENDATION FOR MEDAL STOP

iii)
> O'KELLY WINS WIMBLEDON STOP FIRST EVER IRISH CHAMPION STOP THRILLING MATCH PLAYED TO 5 SETS STOP NAILBITING FINISH STOP O'KELLY 'OVER THE MOON' STOP PLANS LONG HOLIDAY STOP

2 You are a news reporter for a popular newspaper and have been sent to cover a serious traffic accident. Write an article (of about 250 words) for your newspaper. Before you begin to write, ask yourself the following questions:

a) What happened, in brief? Write down all the words you can think of on the topic (e.g. *crash, skid, a write-off, injured, trapped, rescue services*, etc.).
b) Who was involved? Were there any witnesses? Did you get an interview?
c) Did you get a story from a spokesperson in overall charge?
d) Were there any lessons to be learnt for the future?

You may find the Summary box at the end of this unit of help in writing your article.

3 Write an article for a quality newspaper describing an important event (e.g. a ceremony, a demonstration, a fire). Your article should be no longer than 300 words.

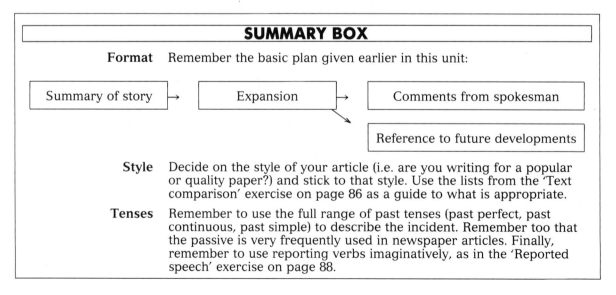

SUMMARY BOX

Format   Remember the basic plan given earlier in this unit:

Summary of story → Expansion → Comments from spokesman

Reference to future developments

Style   Decide on the style of your article (i.e. are you writing for a popular or quality paper?) and stick to that style. Use the lists from the 'Text comparison' exercise on page 86 as a guide to what is appropriate.

Tenses   Remember to use the full range of past tenses (past perfect, past continuous, past simple) to describe the incident. Remember too that the passive is very frequently used in newspaper articles. Finally, remember to use reporting verbs imaginatively, as in the 'Reported speech' exercise on page 88.

Giving a Speech

To start you thinking

Discuss the following questions with your partner.

1 Have you ever had to make a speech? If so, where and when?

2 A speech is, of course, intended to be spoken or read aloud. Are you aware of this when you read the speech? If so, how do you think the writer creates this sense of an audience?

3 Do you know any phrases typically used in speeches in English? Make a list.

A speech

Read the speech below and answer the following questions.

1 Where is the speech being made? Is it a formal or informal occasion?

2 Underline words or phrases which are typically used in speeches.

> "Ladies and Gentlemen,
>
> May I have your attention please! I'd like to take this opportunity to say a few words. As an international organisation, we don't often have the chance to meet each other in person–which is one of the the reasons I have
> 5 enjoyed this gathering so much. It has been a pleasure to see old friends again and, of course, to meet new colleagues too.
>
> On the business side, this year has been a very good one for International Travel and our results have been excellent, in spite of the problems we've had with rates of exchange. All
> 10 this would not, of course, have been possible without your enthusiasm and commitment. I think I can say without boasting that we now have a worldwide reputation for reliability and quality of service. Moreover, we have made a significant contribution to raising standards throughout our
> 15 profession. I would like to thank each and every one of you for your efforts. I feel that we can be proud of what we have achieved.
>
> As you all know, the travel business is highly competitive and no one can afford to rest on their laurels. Market conditions
> 20 can change rapidly and we need to be able to adapt to future challenges. I have every confidence that with our team we will be as successful in the future as we have in the past.
>
> Well, ladies and gentlemen, I won't keep you from your dessert any longer. I hope that this has been a useful and
> 25 enjoyable conference for you and that you will go back with some fresh ideas. Finally, I would like to propose a toast to International Travel. Here's to International Travel!"

Format

Work with your partner to answer the following questions.

1 The speaker has divided her speech into four distinct paragraphs. What is the topic of each of the four sections?

2 Do the paragraphs flow easily one from the other, or does the text seem jerky and unconnected? Give reasons for your answer.

3 The model speech falls into three basic steps common to all speeches. What are these steps?

The language of speeches

1 Find the phrases used by the speaker to:

a) open her speech
b) praise her audience
c) make a modest claim
d) thank her audience
e) finish her speech

2 Tick off the phrases in the box below which you have already underlined in the model speech. Then with your partner, put a cross against the phrases which would only be suitable for a very informal occasion.

☐ May I have your attention please

☐ Could you all just be quiet for a moment

☐ It's a great pleasure for me to . . .

☐ Thanks for coming, everyone

☐ I'd like to take this opportunity to . . .

☐ On behalf of us all I'd like to . . .

☐ Thanks ever so much for . . .

☐ I'd like to wish you every happiness for the future

☐ I hope I haven't rambled on for too long . . .

☐ I would like to thank each and every one of you for . . .

☐ I would like to propose a toast to . . .

Register

The speaker in the model was addressing a business conference and therefore used very formal language. By contrast, a speech made to a small, friendly gathering may be very informal, as in the 'farewell' speech below.

1 Read the speech below and work out who you think is speaking, and where.

> "Ladies and gentlemen . . . ladies and gents . . . I just want to say something . . . can you just listen for a moment!
>
> Right! I know you weren't expecting this, Alison, but we felt we couldn't see you leave without having some kind of a 'do'. We want you to know that
> 5 we're all really sad that you're going and that we're going to miss you a lot – so you must come back and see us whenever you can.
>
> Anyway, we've clubbed together and got you a little 'something' – it's not much but it comes with all our love and best wishes for the future.
>
> OK everyone, time for a toast! Here's to Alison! All the very best for the
> 10 future!"

2 It is important to know the difference between formal and informal language and not to mix the two, otherwise your speech will sound inappropriate or could even be taken as offensive! Look at the table below and work with your partner to fill in a formal/informal equivalent where necessary. (You will find most of the words/phrases you need in the two speeches you have just read.)

Formal	Less formal
a) I would like to take this opportunity to say a word	_____
b) _____	Can you just listen for a moment!
c) We would like you to know...	_____
d) _____	It's been lovely meeting you all again.
e) We've made a collection for you and would like to present you with...	_____
f) a small gift	_____
g) _____	OK, everyone, time for a toast!

Beginnings and endings

There are many different occasions when you might be required to give a speech; it could be for a wedding, a farewell, or when addressing an audience on a topic of interest. Here are the beginnings and endings of some speeches. Can you match the appropriate pairs?

1 As best man, it's my duty to say a few words of congratulation to the bride and groom.

2 As it's our last day in school, I've been asked to say a few words on behalf of the class.

3 I can't let this opportunity pass without saying a few words of congratulation to John and May on their silver wedding anniversary today.

4 Ladies and gentlemen, I'd like to say a few words to you about our work at Dr Barnardo's.

5 I'm no good at speeches but I'd just like to congratulate Jim on his marvellous results.

a) Thank you for listening so patiently – and I'd be delighted to answer any questions you may have.

b) I give you a toast – to John and May!

c) So, well done and here's to your new career! Many years of success!

d) And now everybody, would you please raise your glasses and drink a toast to the bride and groom!

e) Anyway, we'd just like to say thank you for everything – and to give you this little gift to remember us by.

Tenses

1 Look again at paragraph 2 of the model speech on page 91. Can you work out, with your partner, why the present perfect is used in each case?

2 Put the verbs in brackets into the correct tense, present perfect or past simple.

a) I (know) Charlie since he (start) work as a porter in this hospital in 1982.
b) Since she (take up) the post in December, Gwen (make) enormous improvements to the company.

c) You'll have to be patient with me as I (never/make) a speech before.
d) We (have) a very successful year and I would like to thank you all for the tremendous efforts you have put in.
e) When I (learn) that Sam was leaving, I (feel) we just (have to) arrange this party.
f) I (want) to say this ever since I (meet) my new sister-in-law.

Writing

1 This is the speech which Alison made to thank her friends for the farewell 'do' in the exercise on page 92. Work with your partner to build up the complete exercise from prompts:

'I / just / like / say / thank you / each / every / one / you / this lovely surprise. When / Mrs Slattery / ask / me / come / down / canteen / I / have / no idea / what / go / happen.

Anyway, / I / want / you / all / know / I / be / really happy / here. You / be / great / bunch / people / and / I / miss / you / very much /. As / you / probably / know, this / be / my / first / job. I / still / remember / how / terrified / I / be / that first day / ward / but / everyone / be / so / helpful / friendly / I / soon / settle down. I / be / sure / not / everyone / has / same / easy / introduction / nursing / I / have / so / I / like / thank / you / all / very much.

Well, / that / be / all / I / want / say. Thanks / again / lovely / present / and / hope / you / all / keep / touch / me /. I / know / Scotland / be / long way / here / but / if / any / you / get / chance / pop up / we / be / delighted / see you. So, / once again / thank you / everybody.'

2 One of your best friends is marrying someone from Britain and you have been asked to say a few words in English at the reception. Write out your speech in full (about 250 words). You should:

a) open your speech in the normal way
b) say how much you are enjoying the function
c) say a word or two about your friend (how long you've known them, their good qualities, etc.)
d) wish the couple happiness for the future
e) propose a toast

You may like to use suggestions from the Summary box at the end of this unit.

3 You have been asked to give a talk to a local English-speaking club on a subject which interests you (a hobby, a charity, an organisation like 'Amnesty International' or 'Greenpeace' for example). Instead of finishing with a toast, you will of course need to provide a different conclusion to your speech, for example:

GREENPEACE STANDS FOR A SAFE AND NUCLEAR-FREE WORLD. FRESH AIR. CLEAN WATER. THE PROTECTION OF WILDLIFE AND THEIR HABITATS.

Well, I hope I have been able to give you some idea of what . . . is all about. I think I should stop now but I will of course be pleased to answer any questions you may have. Thank you for listening so patiently.

Write out your talk (and be prepared to try it out in front of the class later!).

GREENPEACE

Against all odds, Greenpeace has brought the plight of the natural world to the attention of caring people. Terrible abuses to the environment, often carried out in

5 remote places or far out to sea have been headlined on television and in the press.

Greenpeace began with a protest voyage into a nuclear
10 test zone. The test was disrupted. Today, the site at Amchitka in the Aleutian Islands is a bird sanctuary.

Then Greenpeace sent its tiny
15 inflatable boats to protect the whales. They took up position between the harpoons and the fleeing whales. Today, commercial whaling is banned.

20 On the ice floes of Newfoundland, Greenpeace volunteers placed their bodies between the gaffs of the seal hunters and the helpless seal pups. The hunt was

subsequently called off.
25 In the North Atlantic, Greenpeace drove its turned back dump ships carrying chemical wastes. New laws to protect the

North Sea have been promised.

Peaceful direct action by Greenpeace has
30 invoked the power of public opinion which in turn has forced changes in the law to protect wildlife and to stop the pollution of the natural world.

SUMMARY BOX

Format   A useful way to structure your speech is as follows:

| Introduction/Welcome | → | Body of speech | → | Conclusion/Best wishes for the future/Toast |

Register   How formal is the occasion? Look back to the 'Register' exercise to remind yourself of the differences between formal/informal speeches.

Paragraphing   Remember to begin a new paragraph for each new topic of your speech, and to develop your ideas fully before going on to the next topic/paragraph. (Do *not* write one-sentence paragraphs!)

Language   Check that you remember the sort of language needed in speeches by looking back to the exercise on page 92.

Remember that a speech is meant, ultimately, to be *spoken* to an audience. Try to refer to your audience (*As you all know...*) in your speech.

Describing a Scene

To start you thinking

Discuss the following questions with your partner.

1 Do you go to discos much? What do you like/dislike about them?

2 Describe your favourite disco, if you have one, or a disco that you know of. Where is it? What sort of atmosphere has it got? What sort of people go there? What sort of music does it play?

3 What sort of clothes/make-up/hairdos do people have? (Look back to Unit 7: 'Describing Appearances' for help with vocabulary.)

A description of a scene

A visit to a disco

The 'Streetlife' club was tucked away down a dingy alley at the back of a row of shops. As I picked my way gingerly round the piles of rubbish waiting for collection, I couldn't help wondering if I'd been in my right mind when I accepted
5 the invitation. After all, people got knifed in alleys just like these every night, didn't they?

Eventually, however, the entrance to the club loomed up in front of me. I rang the bell and the door was opened instantly by a rather belligerent-looking man in full evening
10 dress. He was one of those 'body-builder' types – the sort who seem about to burst through their jackets at any moment, 'Incredible Hulk' style. This one was obviously a bouncer as well as a doorman and I reflected that nobody in their right mind would give *him* any trouble.

15 Admittance having been granted, I stepped in from the shadows and was instantly dazzled by a blaze of lights! Multicoloured, they flickered across the dance floor so that the dancers appeared to be moving in slow motion, arrested at regular intervals by a passing beam. And the noise! The
20 whole place throbbed to the insistent, pounding beat of rock music blaring out from loudspeakers placed strategically about the room.

Somewhat bewildered by this assault on my senses, I made my way through the crowd to the balcony, from where I
25 could view the dance floor. At first, all I could see was a mass of bodies, bobbing and twisting to the urgent beat of the latest hit song. Then, as the music faded and couples moved towards the bar, I searched the emptying floor for a familiar face. At last, I spotted my friends, grouped together
30 in a happy circle. They were running through the steps of a new dance routine – with hilarious consequences, to judge from the roar of laughter that suddenly went up. I made my way down to them, although not without some foreboding.

Vocabulary

The words in the left-hand column below come from the model text. Match them with words of a similar meaning from the right-hand column. Compare your answers with your partner's.

1 dingy (line 1)
2 gingerly (line 2)
3 knifed (line 4)
4 loomed (line 7)
5 belligerent (line 9)
6 in their right mind (line 14)
7 dazzled (line 16)
8 throbbed (line 20)
9 bobbing (line 26)
10 foreboding (line 33)

a) moving up and down
b) sane
c) blinded (by lights)
d) feeling of unease
e) aggressive
f) dark and gloomy
g) pulsated
h) with care
i) stabbed
j) appeared out of the darkness

Paragraphing

Answer the following questions with your partner.

1 What is the 'topic' of each of the paragraphs in the model text?

2 Pick out words at the beginning of the second, third and fourth paragraphs which serve to link the paragraphs together.

3 In paragraph 4, pick out any words which link one sentence to the next.

4 Complete the basic plan of the model text below.

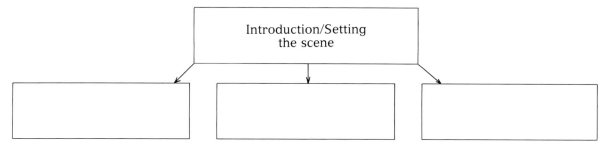

Introduction/Setting the scene

Tenses

Past simple / Past continuous / Past perfect

1 Find examples of these three tenses in the model text and say why they are used.

2 In the passage below the writer is describing the scene in a large household, before the owners depart. Put the verbs in brackets into a suitable tense.

Mr Eugene Foster, who [1](be) nearly seventy years old, [2](live) with his wife in a large six-storey house in New York City, on East Sixty-Second Street, and they [3](have) four servants. It [4](be) a gloomy place, and few people [5](come) to visit them. But on this particular morning in January, the house [6](come) alive and there [7](be) a great deal of bustling about. One maid [8](distribute) bundles of dust sheets to every room, while another [9](drape) them over the furniture. The butler [10](bring) down suitcases and [11](put) them in the hall. The cook [12](keep) popping up from the kitchen to have a word with the butler, and Mrs Foster herself, in an old-fashioned fur coat and with a black hat on top of her head [13](fly) from room to room and [14](pretend) to supervise these operations. Actually, she [15](think) of nothing at all except that she [16](go) to miss her plane if her husband [17](not come) out of his study soon and get ready.

(Roald Dahl)

Using descriptive adjectives

When writing a description of a place, be it a disco, a street market, an examination room or wherever, it is important to make the reader feel that they are really there with you. You may want to describe the sights, the sounds or even the smell of the place, but to do so effectively you must choose your words carefully. The wider your vocabulary, the easier your job will be.

1 Work with your partner to group the following words into three lists: **Light, Sound** and **Movement.**

beat flicker dazzle weave bob glare pounding roar gloomy beam dingy blaring bustling flash drone scurry hum gesticulating feverish blaze whisper

Are there any words which fit into more than one list?

2 Now fill the blanks in the following sentences with one of the words from your list.

a) As he was reading, the light _____ uncertainly and then went out.
b) From the room next door, he heard the steady _____ of voices as the meeting dragged on.
c) The market was a scene of _____ activity as stall holders rushed to get their wares on view.
d) He stood and watched the commuters _____ past him, for all the world like a party of ants on some foraging campaign.
e) The radio was _____ out the latest hit songs and for a moment he was deafened by the noise.
f) At first she thought she was at home in the country. Then she heard the _____ of the traffic and her heart sank.
g) The ships were _____ up and down on the water.
h) Drunkenly he weaved his way down the road, dazzled by the _____ of the street lights.

3 In each sentence, can you suggest alternatives for the words you have chosen which would be equally effective?

Prepositions

1 It is important to be able to use prepositions correctly when describing a scene. Working with a partner, supply suitable prepositions for this description of a boarding house.

Green curtains were hanging (1) _____ on either side of the window. The pussy willows looked wonderful (2) _____ them. He went right (3) _____ and peered (4) _____ the glass (5) _____ the room, and the first thing he saw was a bright fire burning (6) _____ the hearth. (7) _____ the carpet (8) _____ the fire, a pretty little dachshund was curled up asleep (9) _____ its nose tucked (10) _____ its belly. The room itself, so far as he could see (11) _____ the half-darkness, was filled (12) _____ pleasant furniture. There was a baby-grand piano and a big sofa and several plump armchairs; and (13) _____ one corner he spotted a large parrot (14) _____ a cage. All in all, it looked (15) _____ him as though it would be a pretty decent house to stay (16) _____ .
(Roald Dahl)

2 Get into pairs (A and B) to do the next exercise. B should look at the picture on page 101. You are each going to look at different versions of the same picture (a living room). Without looking at each other's pictures, try to find out what the differences are, for example:

Is there a cat on the rug in front of the fire in your picture?

Picture A

Analysis   Read the extract below, which comes from 'Cider With Rosie' by Laurie Lee. As you read, think about the questions on the next page.

The kitchen

With our Mother, we made eight in that cottage. There was the huge white attic where the girls *slept*. The roof was so thin you could hear a bird land on the tiles. Mother and Tony shared a *bedroom* below; Jack, Harold and I the other.

5   *But our waking life*, and our growing years, were for the most part spent in the *kitchen*. Here we lived, not minding the little space, trod on each other like birds in a hole, all talking at once but never I think feeling overcrowded.

That kitchen was scruffy, warm and low. A black grate crackled with coal and beech twigs; towels toasted on the fireguard. On the floor were strips of
10   muddy matting, the windows were choked with plants, and fungus ran over the ceilings. There were six tables of different sizes, some armchairs, boxes, stools, books and papers on every chair, a sofa for cats and a piano for dust and photographs.

When evening came we returned to the *kitchen*, back to its smoky comfort.
15   Indoors, our mother was cooking pancakes, her face aglow from the fire. There was a smell of sharp lemon and salty butter and the burning hiss of oil.

The time had come for my violin practice. I began twanging the strings; my brothers lowered their heads and sighed. I slashed away at 'William Tell' and when I did that, plates jumped, and mother skipped gaily round the
20   hearthrug.

Meanwhile Jack had cleared some books from the table and started his homework. Tony, in his corner, began to talk to the cat and play. So, with the curtains drawn close and the pancakes coming, we settled down to the evening.

(*Cider with Rosie*, Laurie Lee)

---

1 In the description the writer creates a convincing picture by working on our senses of sight, smell and hearing.

a) Which phrases appeal to our sense of hearing? Underline them. Pick out individual words which imitate the word they are describing.

b) Which phrases appeal to our sense of smell? Underline them.

c) In paragraph 2, why does the writer compare the occupants of the kitchen with 'birds in a hole'? What type of atmosphere is he trying to convey?

2 Notice how the writer 'zooms in' on the things he wishes to describe, rather like a film cameraman zooming in on a scene. Look at the paragraph summaries below and put them in the order they are placed in in the model.

a) Evening – violin practice

b) The family evening

c) The evening – sounds and flavours

d) The kitchen – a visual description

e) The cottage

f) The kitchen as communal meeting place

3 The words in italics have a special function in the text. What is this function?

4 A good description often evokes memories of something in your own experience. How far does the writer awaken *your* memories of childhood?

Writing

USEFUL LANGUAGE

to bustle
to bawl
to shout at the top of your voice
a stall
a stall holder
wares/goods
shoddy
second-hand
a reject
top quality
a bargain
to bargain (with someone) for...
to reduce
to outdo someone
to compete (with someone) for...
bric-a-brac
to be taken in by someone/ something

1 Describe a visit to a street market. Discuss the questions below with your partner and make notes before you begin to write. Use the 'Writing plan' to help you if you wish.

Discussion

a) Do you like markets? Are there any in your local village/town? What sort of things do they sell?

b) What time do markets usually open? What sort of preparations go on before they open?

c) What sort of people work in a market? Is there anything special about their dress or their speech? Do you get any rogues? What sort of tricks can they pull (e.g. do they substitute coloured water for perfume or cheat the customer in some other way?) Have you ever fallen for one of these tricks?

d) What are the sights and sounds of a busy market? How do customers usually behave? Are there any 'typical' customers?

e) How does the atmosphere of the market change as the day finishes? What do the stalls/square look like when the rush is over?

Introductory paragraph Background to visit (where the market was/why you were going)

Paragraph 2 Early morning – stall holders prepare for the day

Paragraph 3 The market in full swing – sights and sounds

Paragraph 4 Character-types – stall holders and customers

Concluding paragraph The end of the day – the market at closing time

bride
bridegroom
best man
bridesmaid
in-laws
a registry office
a church/civil
   wedding
a wedding dress
a veil
marriage vows

2 Describe a ceremony you have attended, such as a wedding. You should write approximately 250–300 words. Look at the Summary box below before you begin.

3 Describe a visit to a hospital. You should write approximately 250–300 words.

SUMMARY BOX

Format   Once you have set the scene in your introduction, you may like to develop your text in the ways suggested below.

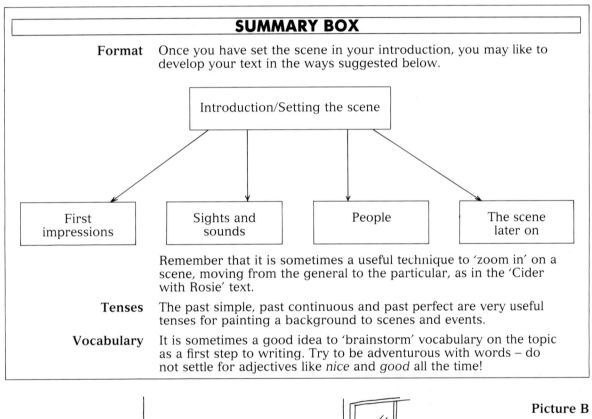

Remember that it is sometimes a useful technique to 'zoom in' on a scene, moving from the general to the particular, as in the 'Cider with Rosie' text.

Tenses   The past simple, past continuous and past perfect are very useful tenses for painting a background to scenes and events.

Vocabulary   It is sometimes a good idea to 'brainstorm' vocabulary on the topic as a first step to writing. Try to be adventurous with words – do not settle for adjectives like *nice* and *good* all the time!

Picture B

Stating an Opinion

'I feel so sorry for them pacing up and down like that.'

To start you thinking

Work in groups to discuss the following questions.

1 Have you been to a zoo a) as a child and/or b) more recently? If so, what was your overall impression?

2 If you have never been to a zoo, for what reason – because you haven't had the opportunity or because you don't like the idea?

3 In what ways do you think zoos might be cruel? Make a list.

An opinion text

Now read the text opposite, which comes from a popular magazine. How many of the writer's arguments against zoos did you anticipate?

Paragraphing

When writing your opinion, it is obviously very important to have a clear and ordered plan in your head or on paper before you write. Each new aspect of your argument should be set out in a separate paragraph. A well-written paragraph frequently contains a key sentence which the writer goes on to explore in more detail in the rest of the paragraph.

1 What is the topic of each of the six paragraphs in the model?

2 Can you pick out a key sentence in each?

3 Look at paragraph 2 and decide how the other sentences expand the information given in the key sentence. Do they:

a) give examples?
b) give a further explanation?
c) give a judgement?
d) do a mixture of the above?
e) do something else?

Examine paragraphs 3 and 4 in the same way.

ARE OUR ZOOS CRUEL TO WILD ANIMALS?

1 Many of us have enjoyed a visit to the zoo and regard it as a fun day out. Seeing real tigers and elephants, especially if it is for the first time, can be an interesting, even thrilling experience. Yet how many people stop and wonder whether the pleasure the animals give to us means that the animals themselves are suffering unnecessarily?

2 It seems to me that no zoo has enough money to provide even basic habitats or environments for all the species they keep. Most animals are put in a totally artificial environment, isolated from every-

thing they'd encounter in their natural habitat. As I see it, this isolation can amount to cruelty. In some zoos you see cages with no trees or foliage[1] - I've even seen cages for burrowing[2] animals like rabbits which have concrete floors. Cruelty doesn't just mean starving or physical abuse[3] - it can be much less obvious than that.

3 Big predators[4] are designed to chase and hunt, and by depriving them of hunting, I believe you are depriving them of one of the main reasons for which they have evolved[5]. The big cats lie about in a zoo because there is nothing else for them to do. Their food is provided for them. And the problem is not just with big cats. Animals like polar bears and chimpanzees too may become very frustrated in a zoo. They are highly intelligent, curious animals and need a challenging environment. Imprisoning them in an often totally inadequate amount of space cannot be right.

4 Zoo supporters argue that zoos provide an educational service, but often the captive environment can be misleading. For example, tigers are solitary animals which like space and privacy but if you go to a zoo you'll often see them caged

together in packs. Zoos may try hard to promote education and conservation to get themselves a better image, but few have a genuine education programme.

5 Another claim often made is that, if we didn't have animals in zoos, we wouldn't see them at all. But we aren't living in Victorian times. Most of us have television and go to the cinema so we know what wildlife looks like. If an animal is suffering by being kept in captivity, isn't it kinder to see it on a film?

6 I appreciate that it would be unrealistic to be against captivity of some kind, if that's the only way we can save some animals. But I'm convinced that there are better ways of protecting endangered species than putting them in zoos. In my view, the focus[6] should be on conserving animals in the wild. If the conventional zoo were to give way to special, protected sanctuaries in the wild, our concern for animals would indeed be demonstrated.

[1]*foliage*: leaves of a tree or plant
[2]*to burrow*: to dig
[3]*abuse*: ill-treatment
[4]*predators*: animals which kill others for food
[5]*evolve*: develop from simpler species
[6]*focus*: aim, objective

Format   A good argumentative text usually includes four basic steps. Step 1 is the introduction. Fill in the other steps in the boxes below in the order in which they occur in the model text.

- Conclusion/Restatement of your views
- Other people's arguments and why they are wrong
- Your personal opinion and the reasons for it

| Introduction/ Stating the problem | → | | → | | → | |

Discussion

Do you agree with the writer's arguments against zoos? Why/Why not?
Make a list of the arguments you would use *against* the writer, and *in favour* of zoos.

1 _____

2 _____

3 _____

4 _____

Keep your list, as you may need to use these ideas later.

Giving a personal opinion

1 Look again at the model and decide whether you think the writer is being firm or tentative about their opinions. Can you pick out phrases/sentences which demonstrate this?

2 Which of the following are a) the strongest and b) the most tentative ways of giving opinions?

Opinion language

I believe/think...
It strikes me that...
As I see it, / In my opinion / To my mind
I feel very strongly that...
I'm inclined to believe that...
I am absolutely convinced that...
I tend to think that...
On balance, I'd say that...
I would suggest that...
I am totally opposed to/in favour of...
It seems to me that...

3 Tick off the phrases which you underlined in the model earlier. Did you find any which are not in the list above?

4 Is it a good idea for a couple to live together?

What should be done with football hooligans?

Should military service be compulsory for women as well as for men?

Is it wrong to eat meat?

What do you feel about these questions? Talk about them in groups and then write one or two sentences summarising your personal opinion. *Remember to use an appropriate phrase from the list of 'opinion language'* to show how strongly you hold your views. When everyone has finished, read out your sentences round the class to get an idea how others feel.

Contradicting other people's opinions

When writing your views on a topic it is a good idea to consider arguments people often use against your case and show why you think they are wrong. The following phrases are useful:

It's popularly believed that..., but...
People often claim that..., but...
It is often alleged that..., but...
People argue that..., but what they don't realise is...
People think that..., but they couldn't be further from the truth.
Contrary to popular belief, it is a fact that...

With your partner, write sentences using the language in the box above, for the following topics.

1 Are we too hard on smokers?
2 Should murderers and terrorists be executed?
3 Should military service be compulsory for women as well as for men?

Tenses

Conditionals

> If the conventional zoo were to give way to special sanctuaries in the wild, our concern for animals would be demonstrated.

We often use the conditional tense to envisage what would happen if our line of argument were or were not to be followed.

Complete the sentences below, using the conditional.

1 Football hooligans aren't treated harshly enough so they continue to disrupt matches.
But were _____

2 People are continuing to smoke so the incidence of lung cancer is still high.
But if _____

3 The government won't raise their salaries so the teachers are on strike.
But if _____

4 We don't have capital punishment in this country so nobody is executed in error.
But supposing _____

5 We burn too many fossil fuels. The hole in the ozone layer is growing.
But were _____

Text correction

1 The student who wrote the following composition has made some mistakes with vocabulary, tenses, articles, etc. With your partner, see how many mistakes you can find.

2 What do you think are the *good* points about the composition?

Should married women with children be discouraged from going out to work?

Today the public opinion looks to be against women with children who work. The people think that a woman can work when she hasn't children but that she must give up her job after the birth of her first child. This opinion is really frequent and particularly shared by men.

Nevertheless, a job can be as important for a woman as for a man. If a woman has reached her professional aim, it must be difficult for her to give it up. Why is this the woman who must chose between her job and have a child?

Our century will prove that men and women have the equal rights and we can notice that as much girls as boys attend universities and statistics demonstrate that females have the same, even better qualities in some fields.

Personally, I think that women need to have professional aims to be and keep a certain independence and to feel themselves useful. I'm not studying to give up my job later. I want to have children and that day I will share my job between my life and my family. In my opinion, it's possible to work a bit little – for instance only in the morning – and to bring up children. Finally, I think that people who say that these kind of women don't love their children have a false opinion because I'm sure that their children are the most important in their life and I would be proud to be one of them!

Writing

1 'Is it a good idea for a couple to live together before they marry?' Write an article for a magazine/newspaper giving your views in about 250–300 words. Check with the Summary box at the end of the unit before you begin.

2 'What should be done about football hooliganism?' Write an article outlining your views in about 250–300 words. Look at the Summary box below before you begin.

3 Write an article in favour of zoos, using the notes you made earlier in the unit.

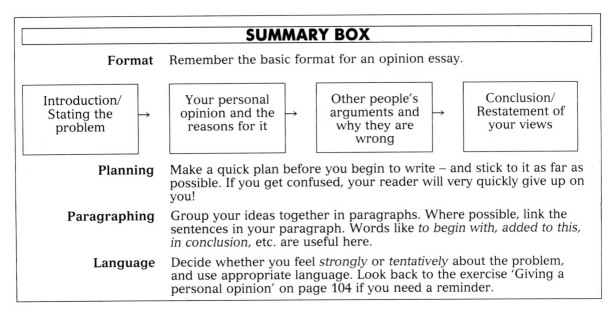

SUMMARY BOX

Format   Remember the basic format for an opinion essay.

| Introduction/ Stating the problem | → | Your personal opinion and the reasons for it | → | Other people's arguments and why they are wrong | → | Conclusion/ Restatement of your views |

Planning   Make a quick plan before you begin to write – and stick to it as far as possible. If you get confused, your reader will very quickly give up on you!

Paragraphing   Group your ideas together in paragraphs. Where possible, link the sentences in your paragraph. Words like *to begin with, added to this, in conclusion,* etc. are useful here.

Language   Decide whether you feel *strongly* or *tentatively* about the problem, and use appropriate language. Look back to the exercise 'Giving a personal opinion' on page 104 if you need a reminder.

Summarising

To start you thinking

1 Are there any nuclear power stations near your city/town? If so, how do you feel about them?

2 What are the disadvantages of using fossil fuels like coal, oil and gas? Is nuclear power a good alternative? Why/Why not?

Vocabulary

You are going to read an article about nuclear power and its possible dangers. Look at the list below of words connected with the topic and write down what you think they mean. Then use your dictionary to check whether your definition is correct.

1 leukaemia
2 nuclear reprocessing plant
3 toxic waste
4 the 'greenhouse effect'

5 radioactive fall-out
6 a nuclear reactor
7 a leak

Now read the article on page 109.

Comprehension

Say whether the following statements are true or false, according to the article you have just read.

1 It has been proved that children who live near nuclear power stations are more likely to get leukaemia.

2 The government believes nuclear power could be the answer to dwindling fuel supplies.

3 Everyone agrees that leaks from nuclear power stations are dangerous.

4 Susan D'Arcy believes that the nearby nuclear power plant was the sole source of her daughter's cancer.

5 Susan is fighting British Nuclear Fuels for compensation.

6 BNFL are paying for research into the causes of child leukaemia.

Paragraphing

Work with your partner to match the summary with the correct paragraph number.

Paragraph 1   a) A group of parents are trying to sue BNFL.

Paragraph 2   b) Child leukaemia is higher than expected in areas near some nuclear plants.

Paragraph 3   c) Only the next generation will know who is right.

Paragraph 4   d) There have been leaks from power plants but the danger is controversial.

Paragraph 5   e) The CEGB and Friends of the Earth disagree about nuclear power.

Paragraph 6   f) BNFL don't accept any liability.

Paragraph 7   g) An 18-year-old girl believes she has leukaemia partly because she lives near a nuclear plant.

Paragraph 8   h) People are asking if nuclear stations are safe.

Paragraph 9	i)	The government is increasing the use of nuclear power for important reasons.
Paragraph 10	j)	Only 1% of the radiation most people receive comes from the nuclear industry.

TALKING POINT

Nuclear power

With our other fuel sources disappearing, do we have any choice about it?

1 For the pupils at Thurso High School, the visit to the nearby Dounreay atomic energy plant in Scotland, was simply part of their course. But to 18-year-old Sharon Coghill, it was much more. Nine years ago, Sharon, who lives 12 miles from the station, discovered she had leukaemia. She believes that the proximity of her home to Dounreay may be a contributory factor to her cancer. There is no medical evidence to support her claim - indeed, two independent inquiries have failed to find any connection whatsoever.

2 But five years ago this week, a government committee found that in the area surrounding some, but not all, nuclear power stations, levels of childhood leukaemia were higher than expected. Today, as then, no one is any closer to establishing why this is so. But says Sharon, "I feel that there is no way we can dismiss the idea of a link and I would like the see more investigation."

3 At present around 15% of the energy we use comes from nuclear power. The Government will probably want that figure to increase to about 20% in the future because gas, coal and oil supplies are dwindling fast - the world's oil supplies may well run out within 100 years. And

burning oil and coal releases carbon dioxide into the atmosphere creating the 'greenhouse effect', the heating up of the earth's atmosphere causing long-term changes in climate.

4 Only 0.1% of the radiation received by most people is the result of discharges from the nuclear power industry. We get five times that from television sets, air travel and watches with luminous dials. 11.5% comes from medical sources like X-rays, and 87% from environmental sources like naturally radioactive rocks and gases.

5 But the question that most people still want to be answered - whether they live five or 500 miles from a nuclear power station - is: are they really safe?

6 There have been leaks from various nuclear installations - including sites dealing with highly radioactive matter - and whether or not these are dangerous is a point of bitter controversy.

7 Parents of children suffer-

Only a bone marrow transplant can save Gemma

ing from leukaemia are convinced of their case. Two years ago, Susan D'Arcy's daughter, Gemma, who is now five, was diagnosed as suffering from leukaemia. They live near Sellafield, a nuclear reprocessing plant near Cumbria, and Susan believes the plant to be a contributory cause of the cancer. She has joined the 28-strong group of parents trying to sue British Nuclear Fuels (BNFL), which runs the plant, for compensation. Twelve of their children have leukaemia, and six have died of the illness. The case is likely to take between two and three years to come to court.

8 BNFL remains adamant that the parents have no cause for complaint. "A number of possible causes, including viruses, are being investigated and BNFL and the nuclear industry in gen-

eral are providing financial aid for this work," says their spokesman.

9 So what's the answer? The Central Electricity Generating Board (CEGB) says that nuclear power is essential in supplying our energy needs. But the environmental group Friends of the Earth regards nuclear power as: "A totally unnecessary and extremely expensive way of dealing with the greenhouse effect - with untold safety problems." It says the solution is to reduce demand by applying more efficient technology.

10 As the argument rages the stakes get higher, with more radioactive waste being produced all the time. Only the generations to come will know who was right. The question is, will they thank us for our decisions?

■Lindsay Nicholson

Making notes

You have been asked to write a short summary of the article you have just read under the following headings. Note down relevant information from the text under each heading, as shown in the first section.

1 The cause for concern

Sharon – 18 – lives near reprocessing plant. Has leukaemia (9 yrs.) Believes plant is a contributory cause. No medical evidence, *but* govt. committee (5 yrs ago) found levels of child leuk. higher than expected in *some* areas (not all)

2 Why nuclear power is important

3 Are radiation levels too high?

4 Parents versus BNFL

5 BNFL versus 'Friends of the Earth'

When you have finished, check your notes with your partner. If there are any big differences, decide if you or your partner should add or cut out anything.

Writing up notes

Read the first paragraph of the summary below and fill in the blanks with appropriate words or phrases.

Sharon (1) _____ 18-year-old schoolgirl (2) _____ nuclear reprocessing plant. She (3) _____ leukaemia (4) _____ years and she believes the plant is (5) _____. (6) _____ medical evidence (7) _____ this but a government committee (8) _____ levels of child leukaemia are (9) _____ near (10) _____ but not (11) _____, nuclear plants.

Reducing the number of words

1 Each of the next two paragraphs of the summary is too long. With your partner, decide on *one* sentence in each which you could leave out without robbing the text of any essential facts.

The government wants to increase the amount of nuclear power we use to about 20% in the future because of dwindling fossil fuels such as coal and oil. In fact, around 15% of our energy comes from nuclear power at present. It is also a fact that the burning of coal and oil may be contributing to the greenhouse effect, i.e. the heating up of the earth's atmosphere, which could cause long term changes in climate.

The amount of radiation people get from nuclear power is much, much less than comes from other sources. Televisions and watches, for example, give off more radiation than the power industry. Yet leaks do occur from time to time and people still wonder if plants are really very safe.

2 The summary is still about 30 words too long. Underline any words/phrases which you think could be cut without changing the nature of the text.

Writing your own summary

1 Now write the last two paragraphs of the summary, using the notes you made earlier to help you. You should use about 60 words for each paragraph.

2 When you have finished, ask your partner to check whether they think that you have a) remembered the important points, b) left out any unnecessary details. If you cannot agree, ask other members of your group what they think.

3 Finally, check through your text and make sure you have written complete sentences, including articles, verbs, etc.

WHY THE FUTURE MUST BE GREEN

World pollution and Britain's contribution

1 Pollution is a catch-all phrase for industrial processes and waste materials which cause damage to the environment and is the greatest threat the world faces. It might be defined simply as 'something in the wrong place', but it is a problem which affects us all.

The ozone layer

2 Ozone is very damaging at ground level, but in the atmosphere it is absolutely critical[1] for maintaining life on earth. The ozone layer encircles the world and protects us from the sun's rays. If the ultra-violet light which reaches us is not filtered in this way, it can cause serious eye disease and skin cancer. Recent evidence has shown that the ozone layer has been depleted[2] by pollutants – particularly chloro-fluorocarbons. CFC's are the propellants which force liquids and sprays from aerosol cans. They are also used extensively in the fast food industry in the insulating foam used to package food.

3 It is an extraordinary thought that something as seemingly harmless as a hairspray or a hamburger carton can pose such a serious threat to our environment, but the link has been conclusively proved.

4 CFC's float upwards and remain in the atmosphere for decades, gradually eating away at the ozone layer. Scientists have recently discovered a huge hole in ozone concentrations above the Arctic ice-cap, and levels elsewhere have dropped by up to 40 per cent.

The greenhouse effect

5 The temperature of the planet has risen only about 3°C since the last ice age; in the next 50 years it is expected to rise by up to 3°C if the present rate of 'global warming' is continued. The result will be catastrophic, with a partial melting of the polar caps and a rise in sea levels sufficient to submerge[3] the greater part of cities like London, New York and Tokyo, and change the world map for ever.

6 This warming process is known as the 'Greenhouse Effect' - a build-up of carbon dioxide in the atmosphere which lets the sun's heat in, but not out. Carbon dioxide emissions[4] from vehicle exhausts alone have increased nearly three-fold in the last 30 years, and the increased use of fossil fuels such as coal, oil and gas exacerbates[5] the problem further. A few simple economy measures, such as cutting back on the amount of fuel we use and insulating our homes better, would help slow the process and save us money.

7 The situation is not helped by the destruction of the world's rain-forests (currently at the rate of 150 acres per minute) because trees play an essential role in absorbing carbon dioxide.

Endangered species - the rate of extinction

8 Species of living things have become extinct[6] for one reason or another throughout the course of history. Dinosaurs endured as the dominant class for over 100 million years, and although the reason for their extinction is not definitely known, it is generally assumed to be the result of a change in climate. Extinction of species has until the last century been largely due to climatic factors, but today it is almost exclusively the result of interference with the natural order by man.

9 Species are now being lost at an unprecedented rate - more than 400 times faster than at any other time in history. Between 50 and 100 species become extinct every day. It is estimated that in 50 years time more than a quarter of all species will have become extinct. That is assuming that the destruction of the world's rain-forests is arrested[7] now; if not, we could lose more than a third.

10 Examples are readily available of species already under threat: 90 per cent of the world's population of African elephants has been lost in the last 10 years due to poaching; approximately 10 million dolphins have been killed needlessly in the last 20 years by tuna fishermen; only 27 Californian condors are left in existence - all in captivity. The rate and threat of extinction has so alarmed London Zoo that it has begun gathering and freezing eggs and sperm from endangered species so that they can be regenerated[8] in the future.

[1]*critical*: essential	[5]*exacerbate*: make worse
[2]*depleted*: made smaller	[6]*extinct*: no longer in existence
[3]*submerge*: cover with water	[7]*arrested*; stopped
[4]*emissions*: gases given off by vehicles	[8]*regenerated*: brought back to life

Now write a summary based on the notes in the box below, in not more than 60 words.

Ozone – critical for life on earth.
Ozone layer protects us from ultra-violet rays (cause eye disease + skin cancer).
CFCs from aerosol cans + packaging → reduction ozone layer.
Hole in ozone layer above Arctic ice-cap discovered. Levels elsewhere dropped 40%.

2 In the summary below (based on 'The Greenhouse Effect' column on page 111) this student has exceeded the 100 word limit. Can you reduce the text to 100 words without losing the basic message of the text?

If the temperature of the planet rises by 3°C expected in the next 50 years the result will certainly be catastrophic. As the polar ice melts, cities like London, Tokyo and New York could disappear under water, which would change the world map for ever. The greenhouse effect is, in fact, a build-up of carbon dioxide which lets the sun in but not out. The increase in CO_2 from cars, nearly three times greater than 30 years ago, and the use of fossil fuels has made problems worse, as well. We could, the article says, slow the process by economising on the energy we use, for example by cutting back on fuel and insulating our homes. We also need to stop the destruction of the rainforests (which happens at the rate of 150 acres per minute) as trees absorb carbon dioxide as part of their life cycle.

3 Write a summary of the final column 'Endangered Species' in about 90 words.

SUMMARY BOX

Rephrasing	You should always make your own notes from the text when writing a summary – do not just 'lift' whole sentences from the text! Leave out unneccessary details like lists of examples, names, places, etc.
Writing up notes	When writing out your notes in full, make sure you have used *complete* sentences with pronouns, verbs, articles, etc. as appropriate. Check the number of words, and if you have too many, see if you can delete words which are not essential to the basic meaning of the text. (You may also be able to rephrase a sentence and reduce the number of words in that way).
Linking ideas	Use connectors, (e.g. *Firstly, Secondly, Added to this, Not only*) to link your sentences where appropriate.
Checking	Give your summary a final check, looking for possible mistakes in spelling, punctuation, etc.